**Making
LINGERIE
and Nightwear**

Making LINGERIE and Nightwear

Nicholas Bullen

MILLS & BOON LIMITED
London . Sydney . Toronto

First published 1979
© Nicholas Bullen 1979

ISBN 0 263 06402 6 (casebound)
ISBN 0 263 06405 0 (limpbound)

Filmset in Optima and printed in Great
Britain by BAS Printers Limited, Over Wallop,
Hampshire
and bound by Hunter & Foulis Ltd.,
Edinburgh

for the publishers Mills & Boon Ltd.,
17–19 Foley Street, London W1A 1DR

CONTENTS

INTRODUCTION

Now that the rage for functional unisex clothes has abated there is a revived interest in uncompromisingly 'feminine' styles. Part of this trend is in luxurious underwear and nightwear. So much so, in fact, that many articles of previously considered strictly as underwear have appeared provocatively in high fashion. Either as just a glimpse of, or blatantly as, outerwear. These fashions have revived the market for exotic and extravagant lingerie, much of which is out of the reach of the average customer due to the high prices of such specialization in clothing.

This book attempts to give many the chance to create their own luxury lingerie by dispelling much of the frightening mystique so often associated with pattern cutting. Although those with some knowledge of pattern making already will find the diagrams easy to use I hope that there will be many who will discover how easy it is to alter ready-bought patterns in order to make themselves a more individual garment. Each section covers the first basics of the pattern shapes and then progresses to more elaborate and exotic designs. However, even the latter models are more concerned with the individual's use of fabric and trimmings to give an otherwise simple shape an air of luxury and expense. As most of the styles are adaptable from lingerie through to day and evening wear, according to the fabric used, I sincerely hope that the following chapters will generate an interest and creativity in those who would like to put more of their own personality into their dressmaking.

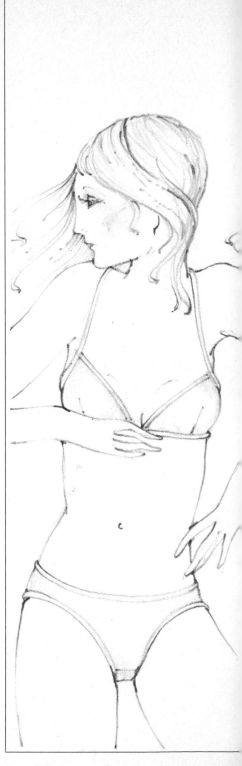

Basic bikini

BASIC BIKINI

Bikini 2

The basic bikini in its most simple form can be adapted for use either as a soft unstructured bra and pants or, equally successfully, as the barest minimum in swimwear. A wide range of effects can be produced according to the fabrics used and the design adaptation eg. cotton jersey would provide the most comfortable and functional model whereas silks or satins trimmed with lace would give a more luxurious and sensual look.

BRA AND PANTS

To fit: 84cm (32in) bust, 92cm (36in) hip. (this will fit size 10 (US 8) or 12 (US 10) but is very easily adapted to other sizes.

Fabrics: For a tight, clinging fit, stretch fabrics are advisable, e.g. cotton jersey, fine polyester and jersey. Fine cotton lawn and silk can also be used, but due to lack of stretch it would be advisable to elasticate the legs and waistband of the briefs.

Stitching information: When using all stretch fabrics a ballpoint machine needle should be used. This prevents splitting of the threads and consequent snagging. A stretch polyester thread should be used with a shallow zig-zag stitch so as to prevent snapping during wear.

Diagram 1

1 Shows the basic bra shape with a simple dart. In order to reduce the bulk when the dart has been stitched it is best to trim the seam leaving a 5mm (¼in) allowance which can be zig-zagged on the edge.
2 If the bra cup needs to be made larger it may be slashed and opened up as in the bikini diagrams on page 17.

Diagram 2

1 To bind the outer edge of the bra cup use a 2·5cm (1in) strip, cut on the bias if the fabric is non-stretch. Press this in half lengthways and stitch to the inside edge of the bra using a 5mm (¼in) seam. This should then be folded out on to the right side and top stitched down.

2 Cut similar strips that are long enough to go from the base of the bra up to the back of the neck where they can be tied or fastened with a hook and eye.

3 Press a 5mm (¼in) seam allowance along each edge of the strip.

4 Fold in half and press so that the folded edges meet. Top stitch together, sandwiching the unbound edges of the bra cups as you reach the lower area.

5 Repeat this procedure sandwiching the bases of the bra cups in a band which is equal in length to the measurement of the ribs below the bust. (The cups can be placed so that they meet at the centre front or they can be spaced out, according to the desired effect.) This can be fastened at the back with a hook and eye. For a tighter fit, narrow elastic can be threaded through this band and if cut shorter than the band it will automatically tighten the fit. A more secure fit can be achieved by taking the front straps over the shoulders and looping them over the back strap (see diagram 2).

Diagram 3

1 This shows the basic pants shape, cut in one piece with only side seams. There can be a crutch seam where the 6cm (2½in) mark is, but this is only necessary where economy of fabric is essential.

If the fabric used is very fine, it is advisable to reinforce the crutch area with a separate panel as in diagram 4. However, this extra panel is often used for added comfort and strength.

2 Press a 5mm (¼in) seam allowance inside on the crutch panel and top stitch onto the main pants shape in the position shown.

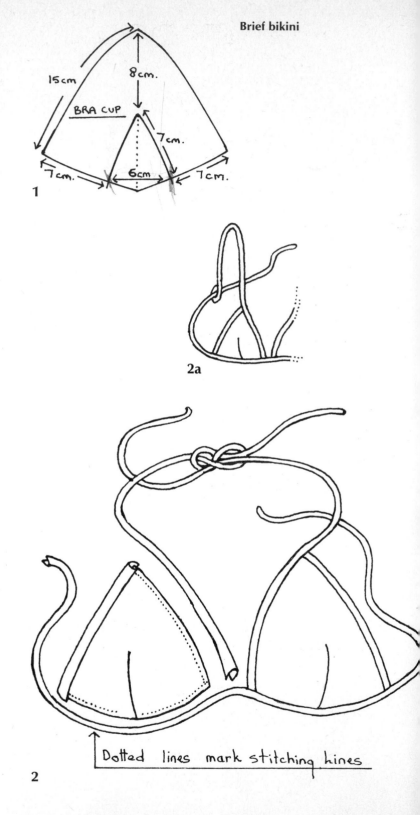

Brief bikini

15cm

8cm.

BRA CUP

7cm.

7cm. 6cm 7cm.

1

2a

Dotted lines mark stitching lines

2

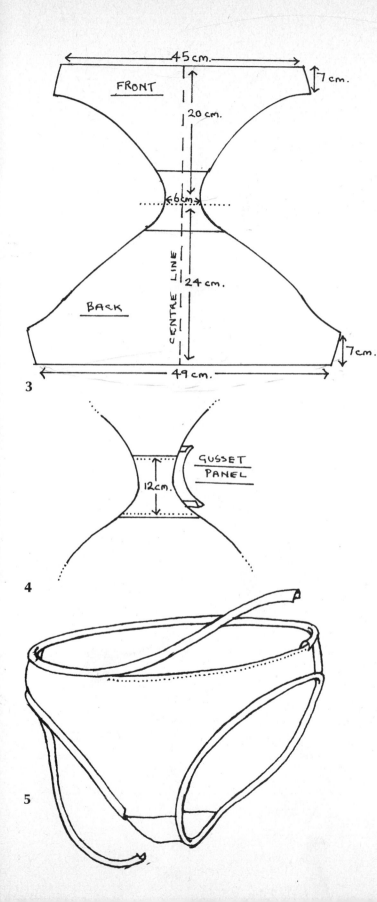

3 Stitch the side seams using a 5mm (¼in) French seam on non-stretch fabrics or a zig-zag seam on stretch fabrics.

4 For stretch fabrics the leg openings and waist can be folded 5mm (¼in) to the inside of the garment, zig-zagged down on the raw edge and then narrow elastic threaded through each channel.

5 For non-stretch fabrics the edges have to be bound with a 2·5cm (1in) bias strip, as with the bra (diagram 5). Elastic can then be threaded through the binding.

6 For the above style it is advisable to make the pants a little larger than one's own measurements so that they are more comfortable. This is done by extending the side seams to the required width—as in diagram 6.

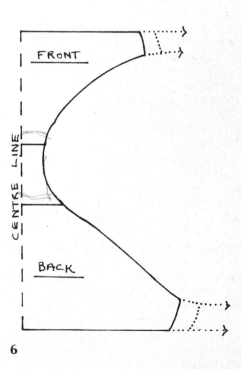

Bikini (2)

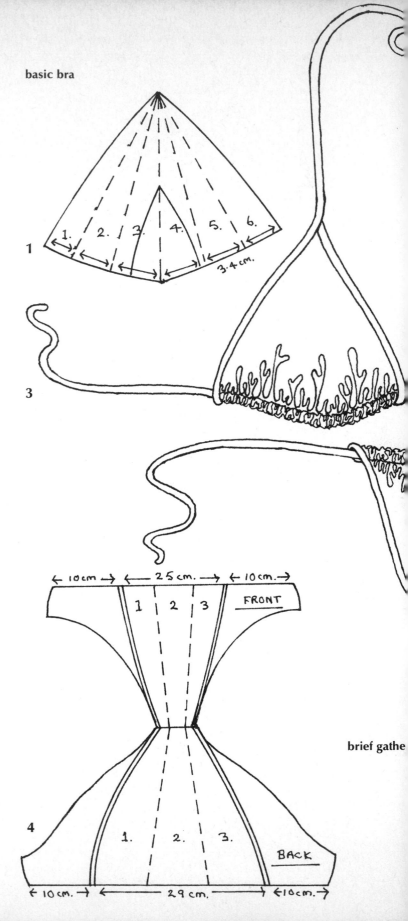

basic bra

1

3

To fit: sizes 8–14 (US 6–12) since the fit is adjustable at the sides.

Fabrics: cotton jersey, towelling, cire, printed cottons (Darker colours are advisable as pale colours tend to become too transparent when wet.)

Stitching information: as for the bra and pants in previous section page 13.

Diagram 1
1   Starting with the basic bra shape divide the lower edge into six equal sections of approximately 3·5cms (1½in). Rule lines from these points up to the tip of the triangle.

Diagram 2
1   Cut along these lines right up to the top point, pinning the point to a hard surface.
2   Open out the lower portions with a 1cm (½in) gap between each. This can be varied according to the amount of fullness desired.
3   Bind the edges as for the basic bra with tie straps round the back of the neck.
4   Fold the lower edge inside 1·5cm (⅜in) and top stitch down. This provides the channel for the lower tie which can be a rouleau band if preferred.

Diagram 3
1   Thread the band through the channel of the bra cups and gather them up to the required fullness. For an interesting look the bindings and ties could be in a contrast colour to the main body.

brief gathe

16

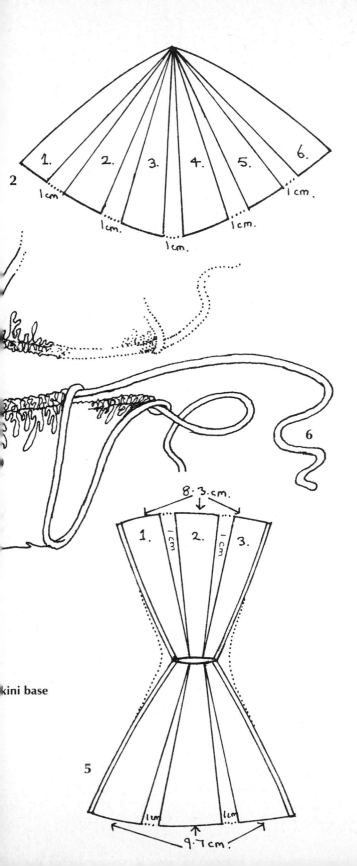

Diagram 4

1 Draw out the basic pants shape as for bra and pants, page 15, marking the new shape of the bikini.

2 Divide the top and bottom lines equally into three sections of 8·3cm (3¼in) at the top and 9·7cm (4in) at the bottom.

3 Divide the crutch line into three sections of 2cm (¾in) and rule lines to connect these points.

Diagram 5

1 Cut out this bikini shape and cut up the six sections opening them out to equal gaps of 1cm (½in) at the top. This can be increased if more fullness is required.

2 It is advisable to add a little more width across the crutch as indicated by the dotted lines.

Diagram 6

1 Bind the two side edges. If stretch fabric is used, however, a 5mm (¼in) edge can be folded on to the inside and zig-zagged down. For non stretch fabrics a tighter fit can be obtained by threading narrow elastic through the bindings.

2 Fold over the top and bottom edges and top stitch a 1·5cm (⅝in). channel as for the bra top.

3 Thread long rouleaus through these channels, gather up the panels and tie on the hips.

17

GATHERED BRA AND BRIEFS

To fit: sizes 8 (US 6) upwards, depending on how much gathering is used.

Fabrics: this design can range from delicate flower printed cottons to broderie anglaise (see illustration) to silk and satin, lace trimmed for a look of exotic luxury.

Stitching information: Since all these fabrics are non-stretch and fine, machine needle size 9 or 11 is essential and the relevant thread for the fabric e.g. cotton thread for cotton and pure silk for silk.

GATHERED BRA

The shape for this is basically the same as the bikini bra, page 14. However, the method is the same as for the basic bra, page 14, except that the cup is gathered into the band under the bust instead of there being a dart. Again the straps can be halter neck or passed over the shoulder and looped over the band at the back. The attraction of this bra will rely on the use of the prettiest and most luxurious fabrics plus the edging of lace or broderie anglaise.

BRIEFS
Diagram 1

1 Using the basic pants shape add extra depth above the waist and around the leg openings (see dotted lines). This can range from 3cms (1 ¼ in) to 7cms (2 ¾ in) at the waist and 2cms (¾ in) to 4cms (1 ¾ in) around the leg. It is entirely up to the maker to decide how deep she desires the briefs to be.
2 Divide the pattern vertically into eight sections, approximately 6cms (2 ½ in) in width. Rule lines between the points.

Gathered bra and briefs

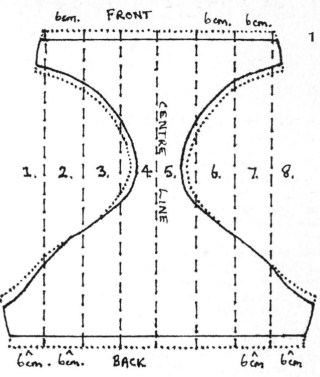

gathered briefs

Divide the sections starting from the centre line.

Diagram 2

1 Cut out the eight sections and space them with 2cm (¾ in) gaps starting from the centre line. This measurement is suitable for sizes 8–10–12 (US 6–10) but increase the measurement for larger sizes.

2 Stitch the side seams using a 5mm (¼ in) French seam or a 5mm (¼ in) zigzagged double seam allowance.

3 Bind all edges with 2·5cm (1in) bias strip (as for the bra and pants, page 00).

4 Lace or broderie anglaise is used at this stage and should be stitched on before the elastic is inserted.

5 Measure around the top of the thigh and the waist and cut elastic for these making each piece 6cms (2½ in) shorter than the actual body measurement. When inserted in the bindings this will produce the characteristic gather and frill on the edging.

See through lace bra

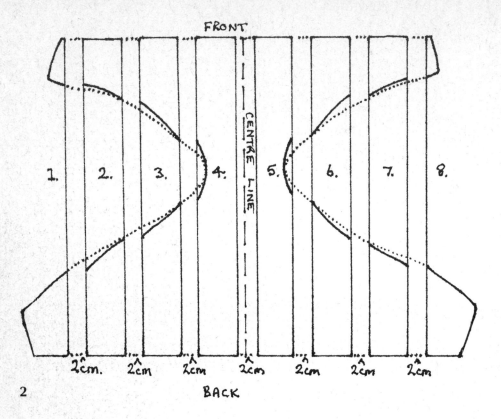

FRONT

1.   2.   3.   4.   CENTRE LINE   5.   6.   7.   8.

2cm.   2cm   2cm   2cm   2cm   2cm   2cm

2

BACK

SEE-THROUGH LACE BRA (see illustration)
This bra could give the most sensual and
exotic look of all if very sheer or flimsy
fabrics are used. e.g. embroidered Swiss
voile, lace, silk, satin.

Stitching information: Use a fine machine
needle, size 9. If lace is to be appliqued it
can either be sewn on by hand, or by
using a very fine zig-zag. If the fabric is
very flimsy it is advisable to mount
fabric and lace onto tissue paper before
machining. This is torn off afterwards.

1   Cut the pattern shape as in basic bra
and pants, page 14.
2   Bind the edges with the narrowest
binding. Narrow satin baby ribbon is
attractive and bias satin ribbon, which

can still be found in a few stores, would
be perfect.
3   Applique the lace as previously
instructed. If an opaque fabric is used
such as silk or satin a very attractive and
provocative effect can be achieved by
zig-zagging a lace motif onto the fabric
and carefully cutting away the fabric
behind so that the motif is transparent.
4   Sew up the dart, cut off the seam
allowance to 5mm (¼in) and zig-zag the
edges.
5   Finally sew on the binding under the
bust and edge with the narrowest lace
available.

Matching briefs can be made in exactly
the same way using the pattern shape
from basic bra and pants, page 15.

WAIST SLIPS
Straight Elasticated Slip

To fit: size 12 (US 10); 92cm (36in) hip (can be adjusted by adding more fullness)

Fabrics: fine cotton lawn, poplin, voile, broderie anglaise, silk, fine printed cotton, georgette, lace.

Stitching information: use fine needle sizes 9 or 11. Mercerized cotton thread or pure silk if the fabric used is silk.

Diagram 1

1   Draw a rectangle – the length of the hip measurement by the length required for the slip. With this method the pattern can be used to fit any size.

2   Allow 20cms (8in) at either end to give slight fullness over the hips. This can be increased but is only advisable if the fabric is very fine so as to avoid too much bulk when elasticated at the waist.

Diagram 2

1   Turn in 5mm (¼in) along the waist line and press. Then fold over again 1·5cm (⅝in) and top stitch the edge down. This provides the channel for the elastic.

2   Press the seam allowances upwards and cover by top stitching a strip of broderie anglaise on top.

3   Sew a frill along the hem line with the seam allowances on the outside. This can be bought already frilled in broderie anglaise or lace edging can be used and gathered up on the machine. Alternatively a strip of ready pleated fabric can be used as an edging. These are not merely for decoration but also give more room in an otherwise narrow slip.

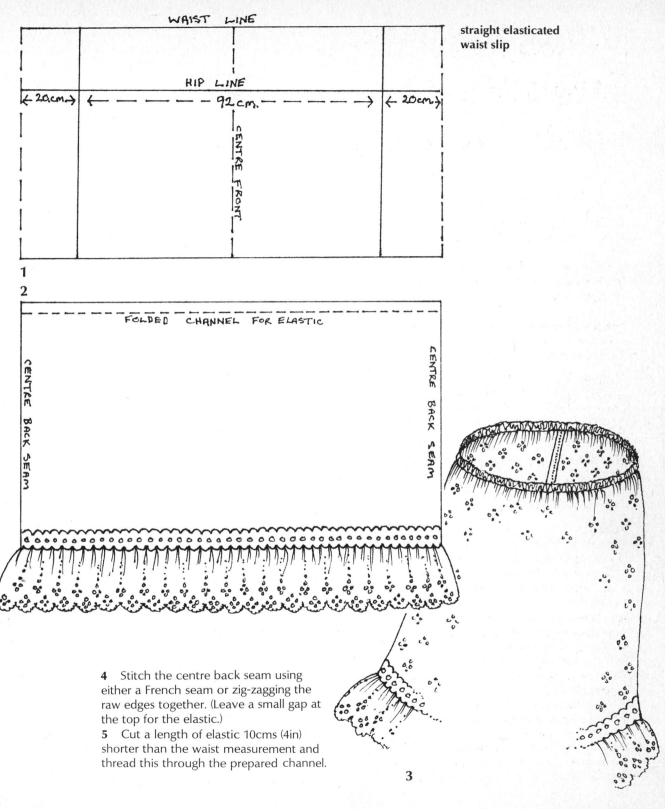

WAIST LINE

straight elasticated
waist slip

HIP LINE

←20cm→ ←————— 92 cm. —————→ ←20cm→

CENTRE FRONT

1

2

FOLDED CHANNEL FOR ELASTIC

CENTRE BACK SEAM

CENTRE BACK SEAM

4 Stitch the centre back seam using either a French seam or zig-zagging the raw edges together. (Leave a small gap at the top for the elastic.)

5 Cut a length of elastic 10cms (4in) shorter than the waist measurement and thread this through the prepared channel.

3

Frilled Waist Slip with Fitted Hip Yoke

The whole effect of this slip relies upon the lavish use of fabrics and trimmings. The more broderie anglaise lace and ribbons used the more romantic and feminine the final effect will be. If very fine lace is used for the tiers, it might be necessary to put a deep frill of gathered net on the inside to give it more body. The prettier the final effect the greater the chance of wearing it on the outside instead of hiding it – especially so if worn with one of the camisole tops featured in the next chapter.

To fit: size 12 (US 10); waist 61cm (24in), hip 92cm (36in).

Fabrics: cotton lawn, broderie anglaise, lace (ready made frills can be bought but flat edging to be ruffled is more economical).

Diagram 1
1 To create front and back hip yoke follow the instructions for the four panel waist slip, i.e. diagrams 1, 2 and 3.
2 The flaring is not necessary since only the hip line is used as the base.
3 A centre front seam is not necessary but the centre back can be cut on the selvedge and used as the opening.

Diagram 2
1 Press upwards a 5mm (¼in) seam allowance onto the right side of the hip line.
2 Top stitch broderie anglaise ribbon on top of this. Narrow baby ribbon can be slotted through the holes if wished.

Bra and slip (see page 22)

Camisole and layered petticoat (see page 45)

Corselette with long, layered petticoat

Strapless Corselette (see page 67)

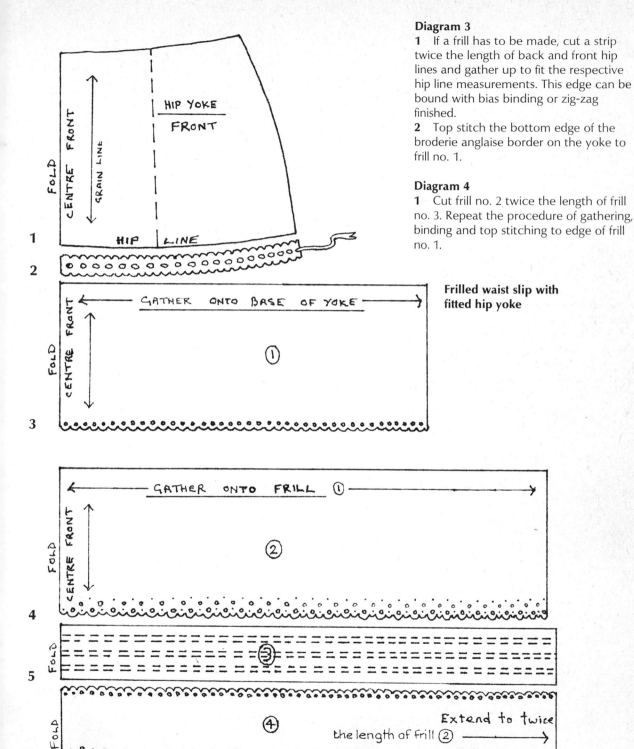

Diagram 3

1 If a frill has to be made, cut a strip twice the length of back and front hip lines and gather up to fit the respective hip line measurements. This edge can be bound with bias binding or zig-zag finished.

2 Top stitch the bottom edge of the broderie anglaise border on the yoke to frill no. 1.

Diagram 4

1 Cut frill no. 2 twice the length of frill no. 3. Repeat the procedure of gathering, binding and top stitching to edge of frill no. 1.

Frilled waist slip with fitted hip yoke

Diagram 5

1 Cut a band (depth as required) the same length as frill no. 2.

2 Machine three parallel pin-tucks of approximately 1cm (½in) (finished) along the band.

3 Press the seam allowances of 5mm (¼in) on to the right side of the band.

4 Top stitch the edge of frill no. 2 on to the top edge of the band so that it covers the seam allowance.

Diagram 6

1 Cut a double edged frill twice the length of the pintucked band.

2 Gather up to the length of the band and top stitch down to it.

3 Having now completed the tiered front and back, sew up the side seams and finish off on the inside with a zig-zag edge.

4 The waistband can be made in exactly the same way as the four panel slip but can be decorated on the outside with ribbon-slotted broderie anglaise trim.

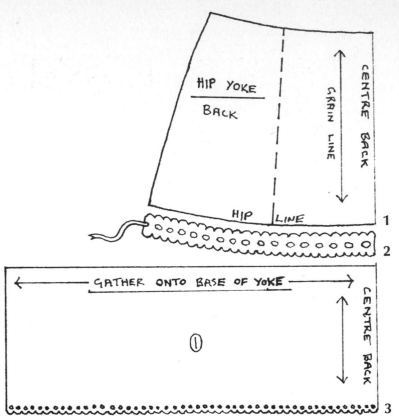

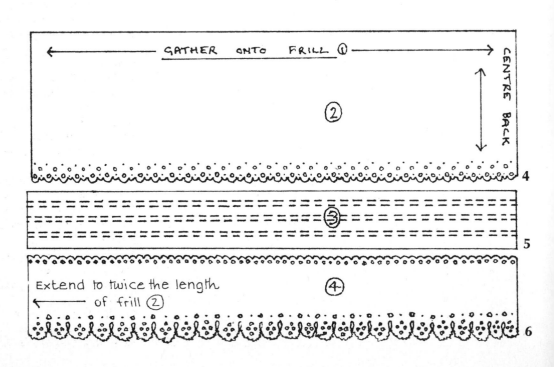

FOUR PANEL
FLARED WAIST SLIP

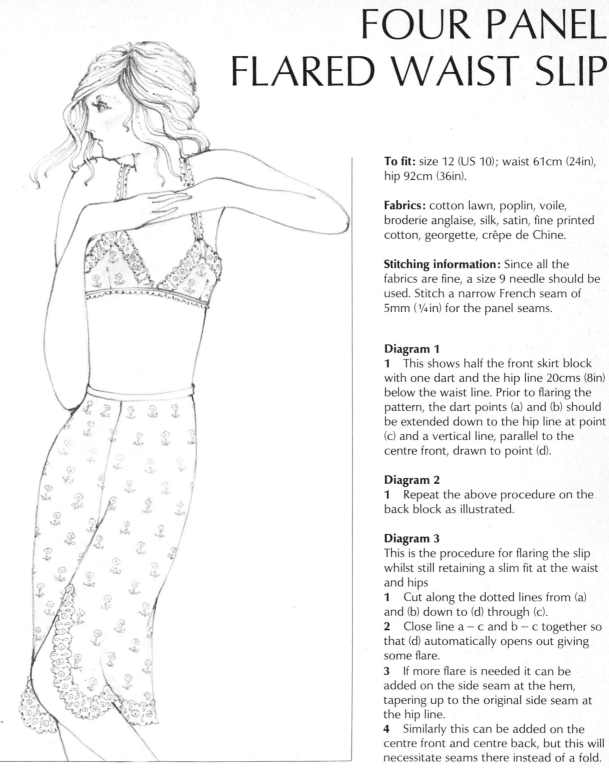

To fit: size 12 (US 10); waist 61cm (24in), hip 92cm (36in).

Fabrics: cotton lawn, poplin, voile, broderie anglaise, silk, satin, fine printed cotton, georgette, crêpe de Chine.

Stitching information: Since all the fabrics are fine, a size 9 needle should be used. Stitch a narrow French seam of 5mm (¼in) for the panel seams.

Diagram 1
1 This shows half the front skirt block with one dart and the hip line 20cms (8in) below the waist line. Prior to flaring the pattern, the dart points (a) and (b) should be extended down to the hip line at point (c) and a vertical line, parallel to the centre front, drawn to point (d).

Diagram 2
1 Repeat the above procedure on the back block as illustrated.

Diagram 3
This is the procedure for flaring the slip whilst still retaining a slim fit at the waist and hips
1 Cut along the dotted lines from (a) and (b) down to (d) through (c).
2 Close line a – c and b – c together so that (d) automatically opens out giving some flare.
3 If more flare is needed it can be added on the side seam at the hem, tapering up to the original side seam at the hip line.
4 Similarly this can be added on the centre front and centre back, but this will necessitate seams there instead of a fold.

5 Gently curve in the hemline and waistline eliminating all angles created by the cutting of the panels.

6 Repeat steps (a) to (e) for flaring the back panel.

7 To create the curved opening as illustrated, draw in a curve from the centre front seam down to the hem.

Four Panel Flared Waist Slip

Patterns drawn in ¼ scale. Size 12 = 61cm waist. 92cm Hip.

Apart from being an attractive feature, it is quite advisable to do so if the slip is particularly narrow so that movement is not restricted.

8 Stitch the side seams with a 5mm (¼in) French seam.

9 A 16cm (6½in) opening should be left in one of the seams, preferably the centre back, but if a two panel slip is made the opening will have to be in the side seam.

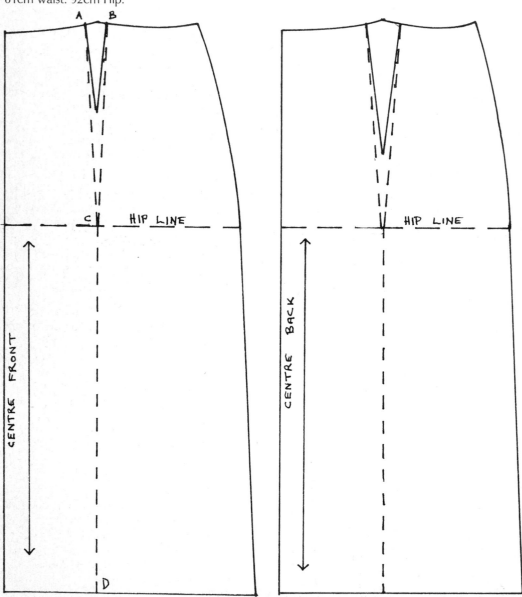

10 Hand roll the opening, folding it back on itself to hide the raw edge. (Zigzag edges can be used but on fine fabrics this often tends to look messy.)

11 For the waistband cut a straight band 6cms (2½in) wide. This should equal the waist measurement plus a 3cm (1¼in) overlap. Fold in half and press and then press inside one seam allowance of 1cm (½in).

12 Stitch the unpressed edge of the waistband to the inside edge of the slip. Press seam allowances upwards.

13 Top stitch the outside edge around the waist enclosing the seam allowances on the inside. Finish with a hook and eye.

14 Press a 4cm (1¾in) hem around the curved opening onto the right side of the garment.

15 Top stitch lace all around the edge to finish off.

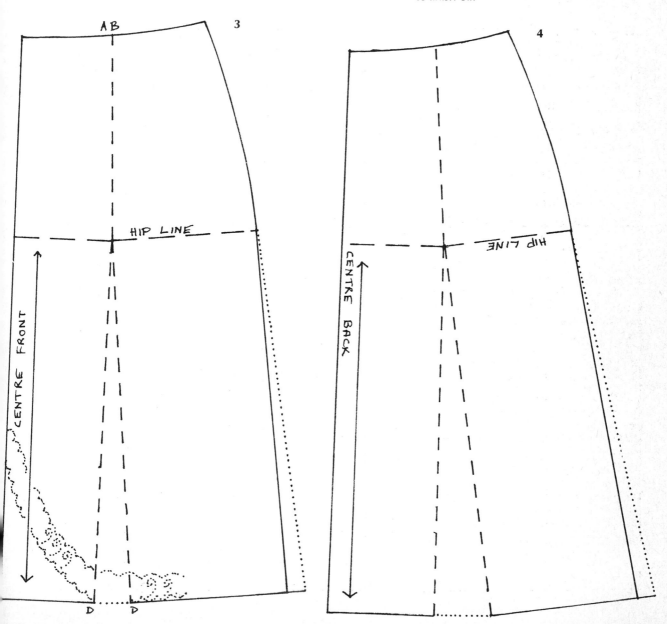

Basic Full Slip

The full slip in its most basic form can be easily constructed by using the basic skirt block from the waist slip section and joining on the bra cup from the bra and pants section. This gives a semi-fitted slip with a fitted bra shape.

Diagram for size 12 but can be enlarged by extending the side seams

Suggested fabrics:
Cotton lawn, printed or plain swiss voile, broderie anglaise, silk crêpe de Chine, satin.

Construction details:
Machine needle: sizes 9 or 11
Thread: mercerized cotton, size 50 or pure silk thread.
Seams should be 5mm (¼ in) French seams with top edge bound as for the basic bra or could be lace edged. If an opening is required this is best put in on the centre back with small buttons and buttonholes or press studs.

1 Draw around front and back skirt block. Ignore the darts in order to give more ease around the waist.
2 More ease can be added to the hem by flaring out the side seams by 4cm (1¾ in) at the base, tapering up to the hip line.
3 Extend the centre front line and centre back line upwards for 12cm (5ins), points A and B. Connect these points with a dotted line.
4 Along line A–B from the centre front, measure a 2cm (¾ in) point, then 14cm (5¾ in), then 4cm (1¾ in) and mark point C.
5 From C drop a line to curve into the side seam of the skirt block.

Full slip, 5 panel with slits

6 From point B on the centre back measure along 18cm (7ins) to D and also drop a line down to curve on to the side seam of the skirt block.

7 Lay the basic bra pattern (with the dart closed) onto line A–C so that it matches up with the 2cm (¾in) point and the 14cm (5¾in) point.

8 Draw around this to give the new curved shape on line A–C and the actual outline of the bra.

9 Extend the centre front line upwards for a further 8cm (3ins) to point E and draw in a gentle curve up to the top of the bra.

10 Draw a 3cm (1¼in) vertical line up from C to F and also curve up to the top of the bra. This will give a fuller, more comfortable bra shape than the bikini look.

11 Repeat the procedure from D up to G and curve down to point B on the centre back.

12 You will now have the three basic pattern pieces for a full slip. The new bra shape can be cut out and the dart reopened. Add 1cm (½in) seams on all edges. If more fullness is required the centre front fold can be replaced by a seam and flared out from point A to 6cm (2½ins) away at the hem.

13 Stitch the dart, trimming down to 5mm (¼in) seam and zig-zag the raw edges together.

14 Sew the bra top to the front skirt panel and treat the seam as in stage 13.

15 Stitch the side seams, finishing with a 5mm (¼in) French seam.

16 Add rouleau straps as for basic bikini bra or just plain satin ribbon can be used.

17 The top edge can now be bound with a rouleau strip as for bikini bra or, if available, use bias satin ribbon.

18 Alternatively, a 5mm (¼in) seam allowance can be pressed on to the outside and narrow lace edging topstitched over this.

Flared slip, lace bra and trim

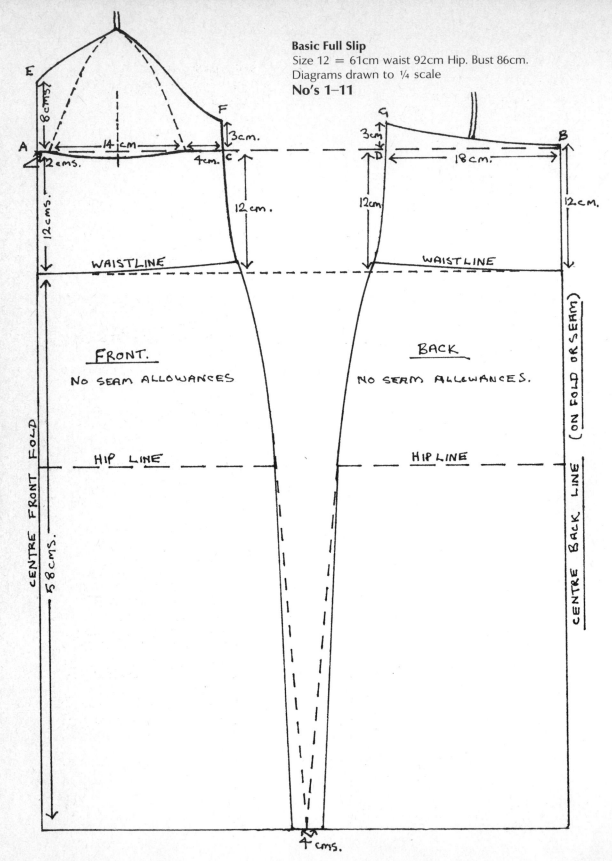

Basic Full Slip
Size 12 = 61cm waist 92cm Hip. Bust 86cm.
Diagrams drawn to ¼ scale
No's 1–11

E

8 cms.

A

2 cms.

14 cm

F

3cm.

4cm. C

12 cm.

G

3cm

D

18cm.

B

12cm.

12 cm.

12cm

12cms.

WAISTLINE

WAISTLINE

FRONT.

NO SEAM ALLOWANCES

BACK

NO SEAM ALLOWANCES.

CENTRE FRONT FOLD

58 cms.

HIP LINE

HIP LINE

CENTRE BACK LINE (ON FOLD OR SEAM)

4 cms.

32

Basic Full Slip
Showing Three Final Pattern Pieces
No's 12–18

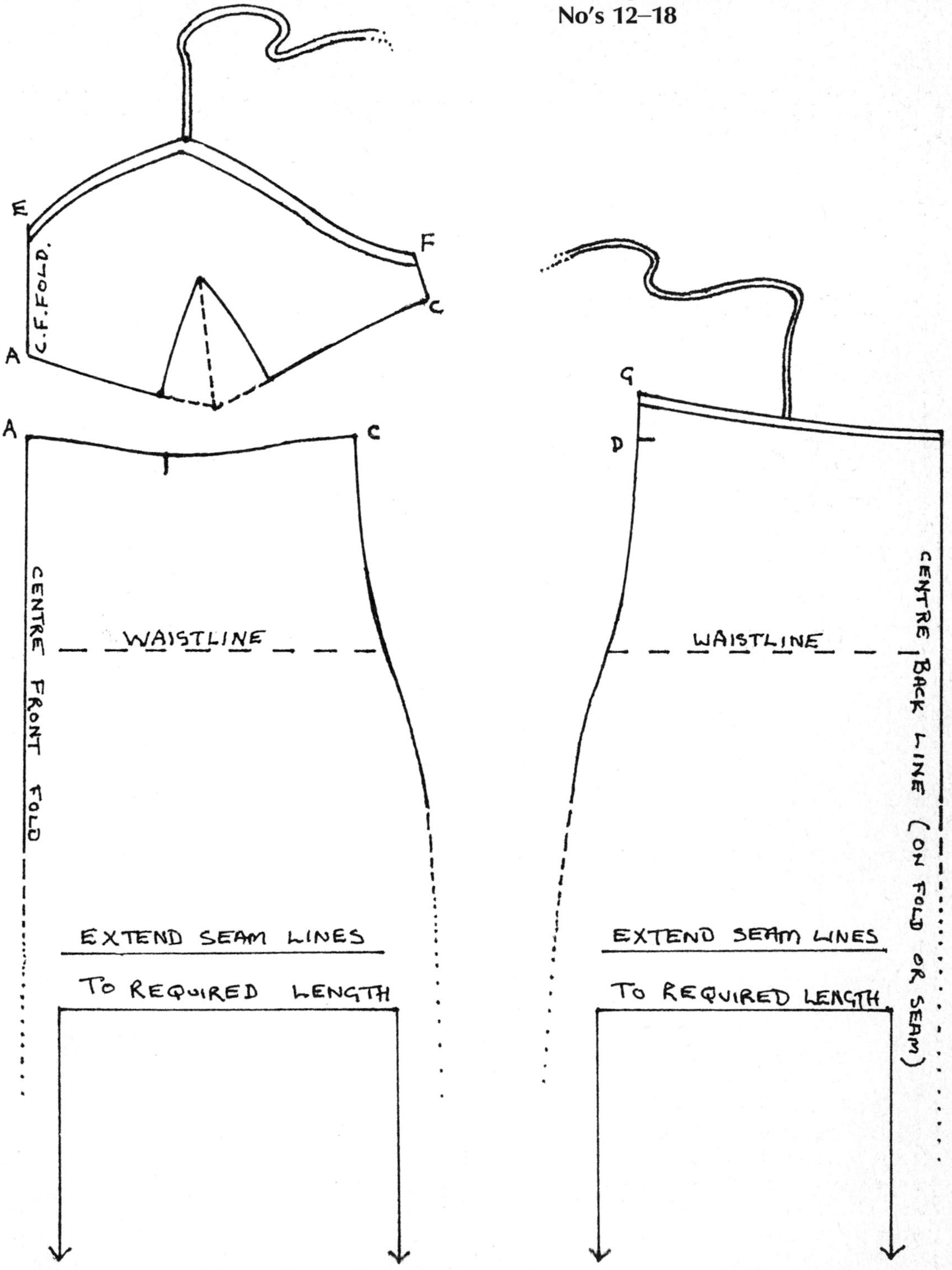
E
F
C.F. FOLD.
C
A
A
C
G
D
CENTRE FRONT FOLD
WAISTLINE
WAISTLINE
CENTRE BACK LINE (ON FOLD OR SEAM)
EXTEND SEAM LINES
TO REQUIRED LENGTH
EXTEND SEAM LINES
TO REQUIRED LENGTH

Flared Slip with Lace Top and Trim

This slip is fuller in the body than the basic slip and has an attractive lace top with a deeper neckline. If made floor length, this design would be very suitable as a nightdress.

Diagram for size 12 but having more flare will fit larger sizes.

Suggested fabrics:
Cotton lawn, voile, silk crêpe de Chine, satin.

Construction details:
Machine needle: sizes 9 or 11
Thread: mercerized cotton, size 50 or pure silk.
Side seams: 5mm (¼in) French seams or zigzag 5mm (¼in) raw edges. If very fine lace is used for the top it would be advisable to mount it onto matching coloured net.

1 Trace out front and back panels of basic slip, cutting along lines A–C and D–B so that the top of the slip becomes separate at the back as well as the front.
2 Divide the hip line equally into four parts on the front and back.
3 Rule parallel lines to centre front and centre back through these points from top to hem line.
4 Cut along these lines from the hem up to the top but do not separate at the top.
5 Pin the centre front panel so that it is stationary and then open up the other panels so that there is a gap of 5cm (2ins) between each one at the hem. You will now find that the hem curves upwards, consequently the curve at the top is accentuated.

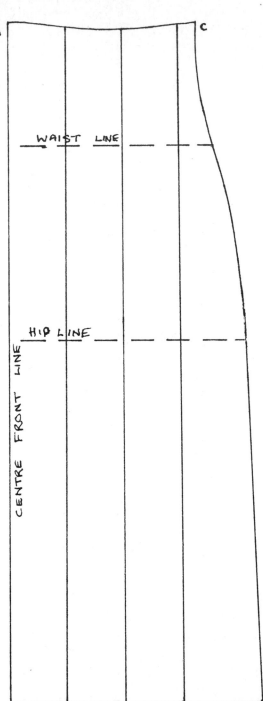

Flared Slip With Lace Top and Trim
Sizing as for basic slip. Diagrams ¼ scale.
No's 1–6

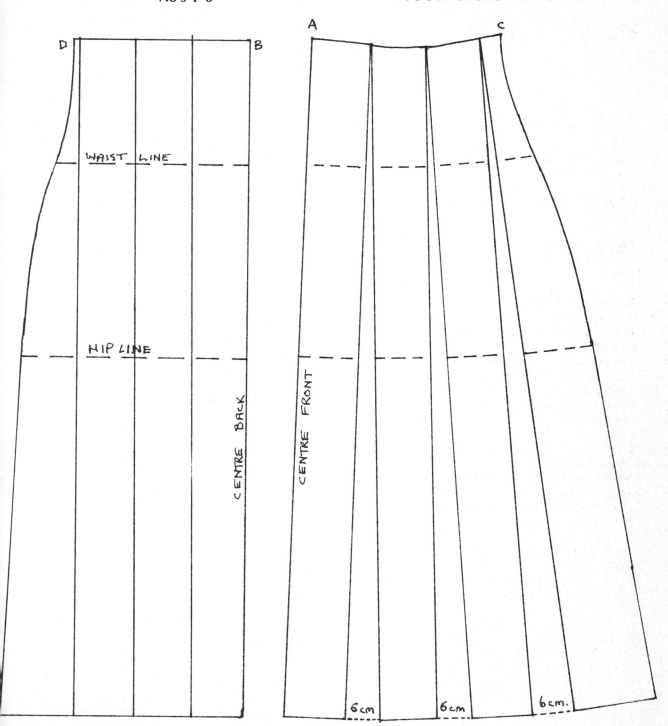

35

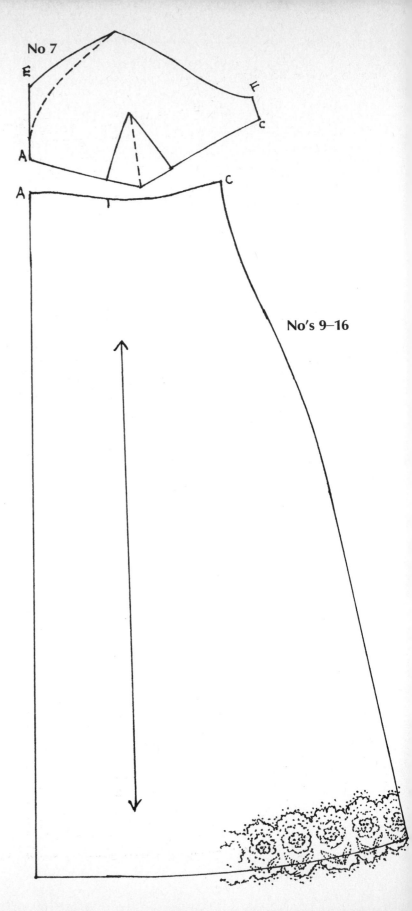

6 Repeat this procedure for the back. If there is to be no centre front or centre back seam the grain line should be parallel to centre front or centre back. However, if the skirt is to have four panels the grain line should run down the centre of the pattern.

7 To give a deeper neckline draw a curved line from the top of the bra down to A.

8 Deepen the back portion of the top by curving G to H, the latter being 3cm (1¼in) up from B.

9 Cut out the two parts of the bra in lace. If possible cut around the motifs of the lace to form the edge, but if the lace is too fine a separate lace edging will have to be used.

10 Stitch the darts in the bra front, trim to 5mm (¼in) and zigzag the two edges together.

11 Repeat for the side seams of lace.

12 Stitch side seams of skirt panels with 5mm (¼in) French seams.

13 Add bra top to skirt finishing off with a 5mm (¼in) zigzag edge.

14 Narrow ribbon shoulder straps can be added, edged with fine lace.

15 Press up a 5mm (¼in) hem onto outside of garment.

16 Topstitch down wide lace edging over this with a zigzag stitch so that the lower lace edging is below the fabric of the skirt.

Flared Lace Trimmed Slip **No 8**

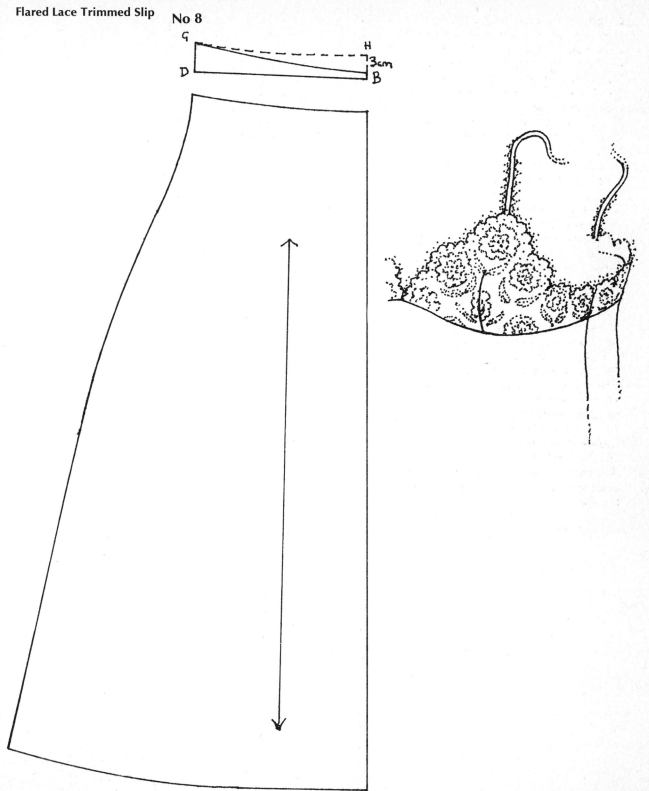

Shaped Seven Panel Slip, Lace Edged with Slit Skirt

This slip, based on the original basic slip, now has been divided into seven panels to produce a fitted waist but still a flared skirt – ideal for wearing underneath fitted clothes. The top and slits can be edged in lace for a more luxurious effect.

Size 12 scale drawing but for larger sizes the waist darts can be decreased and the side seams increased according to the measurements of the individual customer.

Suggested fabrics:
Jap silk, silk crêpe de Chine, satin, Swiss voile, cotton lawn.

Construction details:
Machine needle: sizes 9 or 11
Thread: mercerized cotton or pure silk thread. Seams should ideally be French seams, 5mm (¼in), finished. The lace can either be topstitched on or zigzagged on and the fabric cut away from underneath for a 'see-through' effect.

1   Draw out shapes for back and front from basic full-slip shape.
2   Mark in waist darts from positions for the four panel flared waist slip pattern.
3   From the centre of the dart rule a line, parallel to centre front and centre back from top to bottom of the panel AB to CD.
4   Rule lines from the outside of the darts at the waist up to points A and C.

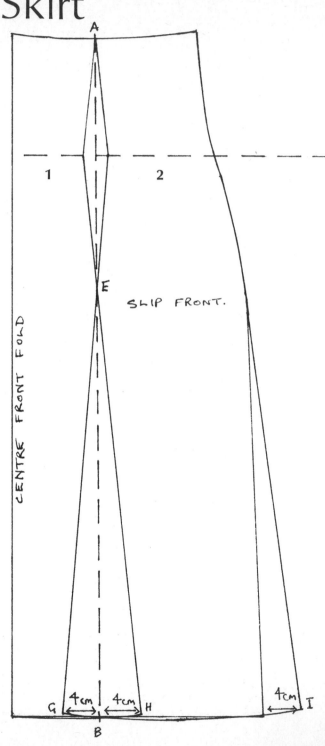

Shaped Seven Panel Slip, Lace Edged With Slit Panelled Skirt
Sizing as for basic slip. Size 12 (no seam allowances)

No's 1–7

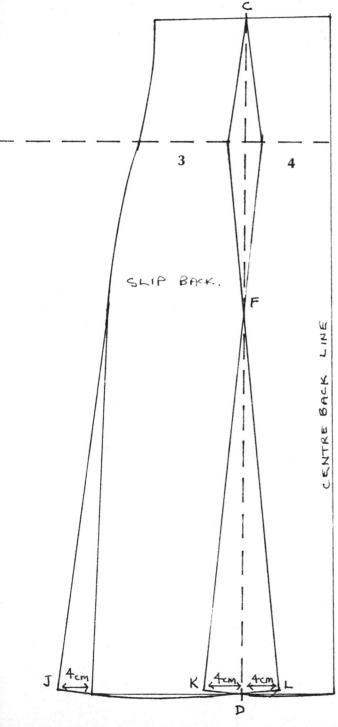

5 To add the flare at the hem measure 4cm (1¾in) either side of line AB, the side seams and line CD to give points G, H, I, J, K and L. (This can be increased according to how full the effect of the hem is required.) These points should measure exactly the same length as from waist to hem centre front and centre back.

6 Rule lines by continuing the waist darts down to points G, H, I, J, K and L. If the measurements of these lines equal those of centre front and centre back waist to hem, they should fall slightly short of the original straight hem line.

7 At all the aforementioned points the hem line angle should start at a right angle and then curve round to meet the original hem line. (So that when the panels are sewn together, the hem should be a continuous curve and not end in angled points at each seam.)

8 Trace off the separate panels 1, 2, 3 and 4. (One being on the fold to produce eventually seven individual panels with a centre back seam and opening).

9 Eliminate the angles of the darts at the waistline by gently curving the seam lines of the panels.

10 Add a 2cm (¾in) extension to the centre back for a length of 20cm (8ins) for the opening. This can be accomplished with small buttons and buttonholes or press studs (a zip would be too heavy for this type of garment).

11 The bra cup and back top of garment are as for the flared slip with lace top and trim.

12 Stitch all the seams of the panels with 5mm (¼in) French seams leaving 20cm (8ins) slits at the hem. These can be straight as in 1 and 2 or curved as in 3 and 4. Also, the length of the slit can be varied according to taste.

13 Press a 5mm (¼in) seam allowance around the hem on to the outside and topstitch lace down to cover this or zigzag lace on to the top of the fabric and then cut away the fabric to the edge of the stitching for a 'see-through' effect.

14 Stitch the dart of the bra front. Trim off to 5mm (¼in) and zigzag the raw edges together.

15 Sew side seams of bodice top with a 5mm (¼in) French seam.

16 Applique lace around top edge of bodice, either by topstitching down on to the fabric or zigzagging down on to fabric and then cutting the fabric away underneath. For extra strength on the edge, fine lace edging can be topstitched all the way round the top edge.

17 Sew bodice top to panelled skirt, trim down to 5mm (¼in) and zigzag two edges together.

18 Press in 2cm (¾in) button wrap on centre back and affix fastenings as to preference.

19 Topstitch narrow ribbon shoulder straps edged with fine lace (the length should be measured on the client).

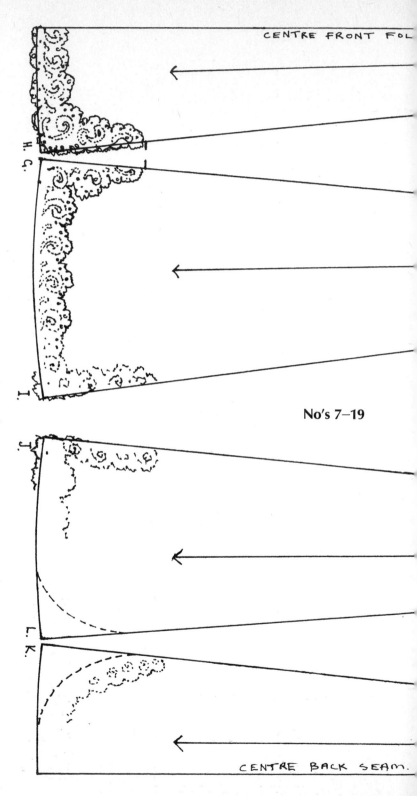

CENTRE FRONT FOL

No's 7–19

CENTRE BACK SEAM.

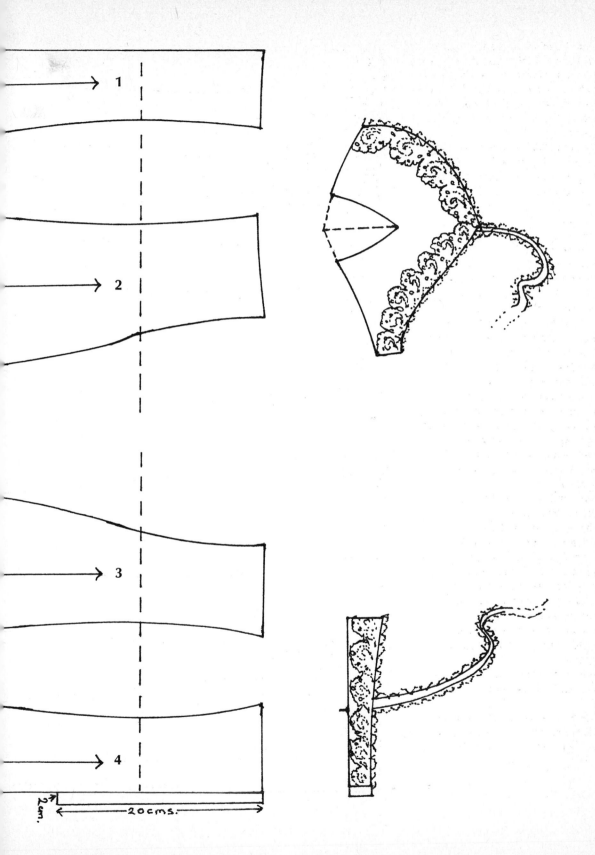

1

2

3

4

2 cm.

←———— 20 cms. ————→

Slip with Gathered Top and Deep Side Slits

This slip can be ultimate in luxurious appeal with its gently gathered bra and provacative slits up to the thigh. A slim petticoat too, so can be worn under tight fitting clothes. If made full length in silk it would be the most luxurious and sensual of nightdresses.

Diagram for size 12 but could easily accommodate a larger figure if the side seams were extended since the bust is gathered and, therefore, more adaptable.

Suggested fabrics:
Satin, silk, crêpe de Chine, Swiss voile.

Construction details:
Machine needle: sizes 9 or 11
Thread: Pure silk thread
Side seams: 5mm (¼in) French seams. Lace can be topstitched on like an outside facing or zigzagged down and the fabric cut away from behind for a 'see-through' look.

1 Draw around the Basic Slip shape with the top, waist and hip construction lines A, B and C.
2 To construct the point in the front, extend the centre front line upwards for 4cm (1¾in) to give point D.
3 From point D curve the line downwards into the concave curve of the front panel.
4 Using the same shaped cup as in the Seven Panel Slip divide it by ruling seven lines from the top, starting through the centre of the dart, radiating out either side.
5 These should then be cut from the base up to the top but not right the way through the point.

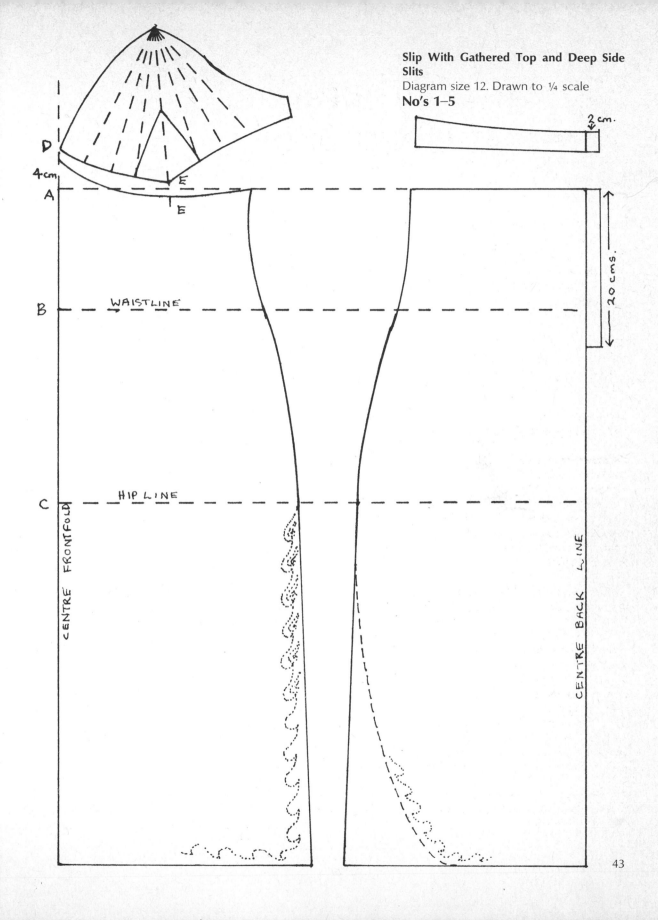

Slip With Gathered Top and Deep Side Slits
Diagram size 12. Drawn to ¼ scale
No's 1–5

2 cm.

D

4cm

A

E

E

20 cms.

B   WAISTLINE

C   HIP LINE

CENTRE FRONT FOLD

CENTRE BACK LINE

43

6 Open these up so that each gap measures 1cm (½in) at the bottom. (This will provide the gathered fullness instead of a dart.)

7 Redraw around the shape gently curving the lines down to point E to add more fullness.

8 Measure 4cm (1¾in) from D to F and redraw the cutting line (double line on diagram). This is necessary since 4cm (1¾in) has already been added to the centre front skirt panel.

9 The side slits can either be rectangular as in the illustration for the front or curved and more daring as in the illustration for the back.

10 Cut out the four pattern pieces with the front panel on the fold and the centre back on the selvege if a centre back opening is required.

11 Run a gathering thread 1cm (½in) in from the lower edge of the bra cups.

12 Gather up to match the measurement of the front panel with point E's matching. **It is advisable before doing this to run a row of tight stitching 1cm (½in) in on the curve of the front panel to prevent this from stretching.**

13 Stitch gathered cups to front panel, trimming the seam down to 5mm (¼in) and zigzagging the two raw edges together.

14 Stitch back bodice to back panel and finish off seams as above.

15 If there is to be a centre back opening stitch the back seam with a French seam up to the opening. Buttons or press studs can be used as fastenings.

16 Stitch side seams to top of slit using 5mm French seams.

18 Around top edge of bra and all around the hem press a 5mm (¼in) hem to the right side and topstitch lace edging over this to cover the raw edge. (If lace is to be zigzagged on and the fabric cut away from underneath there is no need to press out the seam allowances. Just mount the lace on top of the fabric with the outside edges flush. Zigzag with a tiny stitch all round the inner edge then just cut the fabric away right up to the stitching from underneath.)

19 Topstitch narrow ribbon shoulder straps to bra, cut to the required measurement.

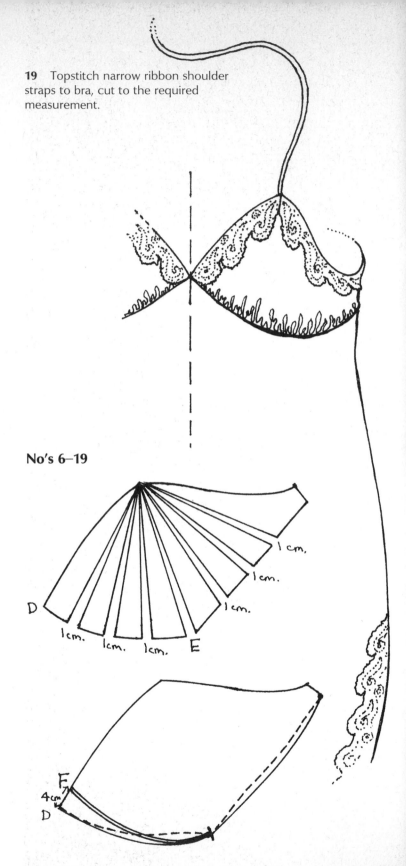

No's 6–19

44

CAMISOLE TOPS

The camisole has been the most basic item of women's underwear ever since the early eighteenth century. Originally known as a chemise, this simple slip varied in form according to the style of dress under which it was to be worn. Varying from a complete dress in the unstructured period of the early nineteenth century until the tight corsets of the Victorian and Edwardian eras when it diminished to the shape of a camisole. The revival of Victorian-style underwear in the 1970s has again made the camisole an attractive undergarment, especially when interpreted in delicate, lace-trimmed fabrics, makes a delightful top for summer or evening wear.

Basic Gathered 'Tube' Shaped Camisole

Size 12, but can be adapted to smaller or larger sizes

Suggested fabrics:
Only the finest fabrics should be used to avoid this garment from becoming too bulky and unflattering, e.g. cotton lawn, printed or plain; embroidered Swiss voile; silk; crêpe de Chine; broderie anglaise.

Construction details:
Since this garment can be in one piece there is no need for side seams but if needed the smallest French seams should be used.
Machine needle: size 9 or 11
Thread: pure silk or mercerized cotton, size 50

1 Cut rectangle of fabric 100cm (25ins) long by 40cm (16ins) deep. If the fabric is very fine the length can be increased to give more fullness. (For larger or smaller sizes the bust should be measured and then 12cm (5ins) added for the fullness.)
2 At either end, which will be the centre front opening, fold in 5mm (¼in) turning. Press, then fold in 5mm (¼in) again so that no raw edge is visible. Machine down.
3 Press on to the outside a 5mm (¼in) turning along top and bottom edge and then topstitch down a lace edging. This can vary in depth according to taste but the top one should be narrower than on the hem.
4 Topstitch narrow satin baby ribbon along top edge leaving an extra 20cm (8ins) at each end for tying in a bow at the front.
5 Measure above the bust under the arms and cut narrow elastic 10cm (4ins) shorter than this measurement.

Basic gathered camisole

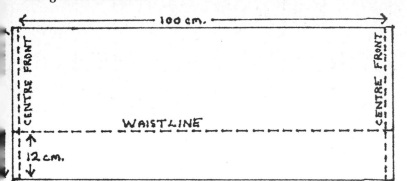

1, 2

3, 4

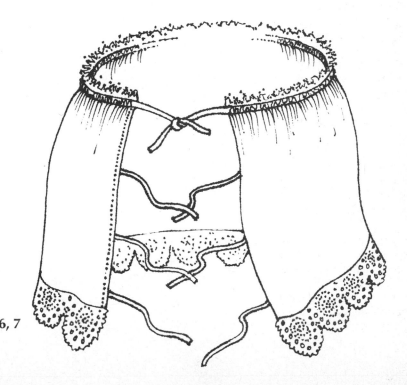

5, 6, 7

6 Thread this through, underneath the ribbon (using a bobbypin or hairgrip) and catch down at the centre front.

7 To fasten the rest of the centre front, 10cm (4ins) ties of ribbon can be used or, for a tighter closed effect, small pearl buttons and button holes can be used.

This garment produces a pretty smock effect which can be worn loose or tucked in. If a waisted effect is desired a channel of ribbon should be topstitched down along the waistband and the elastic procedure repeated as for stages 4–5.

Camisole with Shaped Top, Shoulder Straps and Drawstring Waist

Diagram shows the correct measurements for size 12, but larger sizes can be accommodated for by extending the side seams, i.e. measure around the bust and if, for example, this is 8cm (3¾ ins) larger, divide this by four. Hence 2cm (¾ in) should be added on each side seam.

NB Fabrics and construction details as for *basic camisole*.

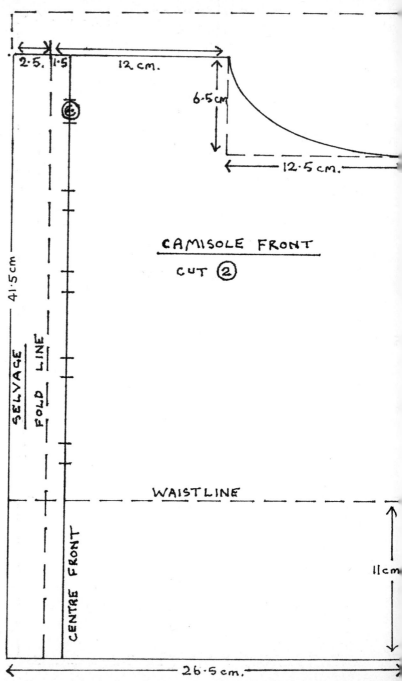

CAMISOLE FRONT

CUT ②

Camisole Top With Shaped Bodice
Includes 1·5cm side seams
5mm all other seams.

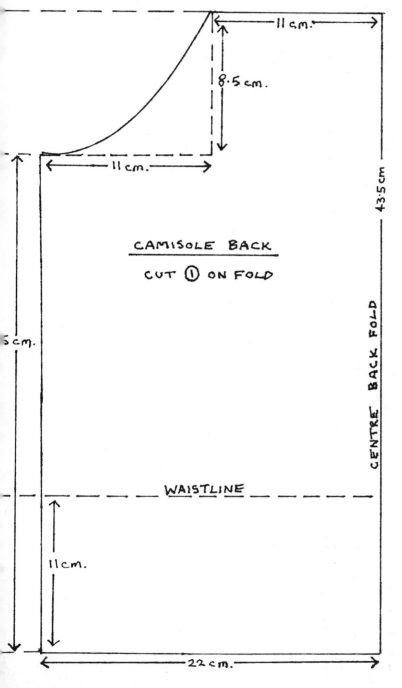

CAMISOLE BACK

CUT ① ON FOLD

WAISTLINE

CENTRE BACK FOLD

11 cm.

8.5 cm.

11 cm.

43·5 cm

5 cm.

11 cm.

22 cm.

1   Cut out two pattern pieces as in diagram (selvege on front).
2   Stitch side seams with 5mm (¼in) seams on right side.
3   Trim down so that the resulting French seam should be 5mm (¼in) finished on the inside.
4   Press in button wrap along fold line.
5   Press 5mm (¼in) seam allowance along top edge, around armhole and along hem onto right side.
6   Topstitch band of broderie anglaise* along waistline finishing 3cm (1¼in) away from folded front.
7   Cut two 30cm (12ins) shoulder straps in broderie anglaise ribbon and insert narrow baby ribbon through the slits in the straps (these can be made longer or shorter as to size).
8   Pin the straps in position on the corners of the back and front.
9   Topstitch broderie anglaise frill along the top edge with the frill pointing upwards and the lower edge covering the outside seam allowance.
10   Repeat the same procedure along the hem but with the frill pointing downwards.
11   If wished these frills can be accentuated by topstitching baby ribbon along the seam edge.

*If a particularly fine fabric is used, broderie anglaise could be too heavy a trimming. Hence it would be advisable to use a fine lace frill for edging and narrow bands of lace ribbon for the straps and waist. If this is used, the satin ribbon can be stitched behind the lace on the straps and threaded underneath the topstitched lace along the waistline.

12 Mark buttonholes as shown and machine using as small zigzag as possible.

13 Finally, thread baby ribbon through the broderie anglaise at the waist to create a drawstring to tie in a bow at the front.

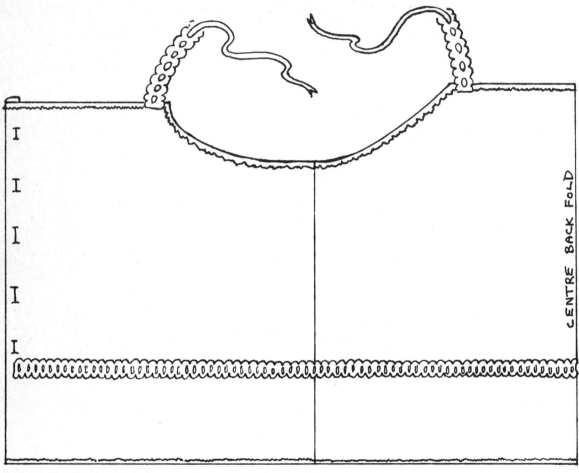

2, 3, 4, 5, 6, 7, 8

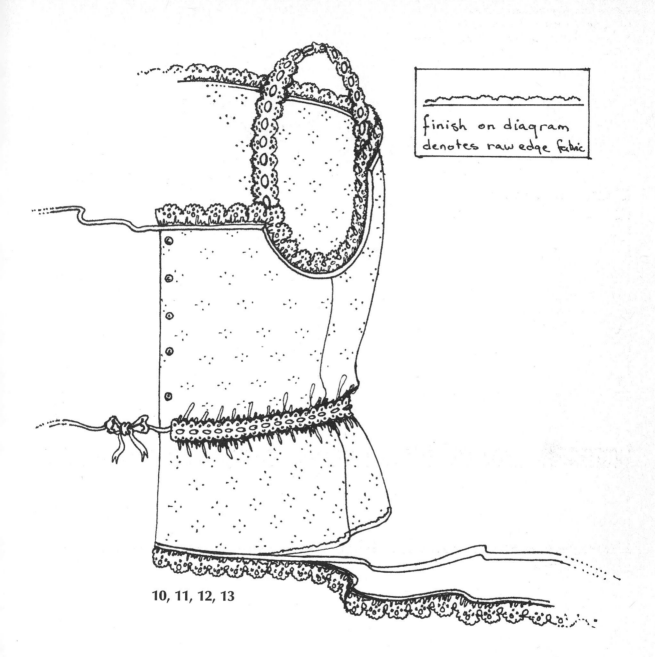

finish on diagram
denotes raw edge fabric

10, 11, 12, 13

Lace Camisole

Suitable for evening or summer wear. Design shown as for size 12, but can be adapted to a larger size using the same method as for the previous camisole.

Suggested fabrics
Cotton lace (as sold for sheer curtains), dress lace, lurex, embroidered lace, printed or embroidered chiffon, antique lace.

Construction details:
Machine needle: size 9 or 11
Thread: pure silk or mercerized cotton, size 50.
For chiffon use minute French seams of 5mm (¼in).
For lace a seam of 5mm (¼in) with the two edges zigzagged together.

1 Draw out the pattern shape as for previous camisole, using the same proportions and measurements.
2 Draw in new bra shape for the front as shown in diagram.
3 Cut out and stitch side seams, the latter executed according to the fabric used.
4 Fold back button wrap. It is advisable to mount matching coloured cotton tape inside the wrap for added strength for the buttonholes and buttons*
5 Press out on to right side a 5mm (¼in) seam allowance all the way round the top and the hem.
6 Edge stitch narrow cotton tape along the waistline on the inside.

*If the blouse is to be worn for evening and fabric has been used with some glitter in it, try to find special buttons e.g. jewelled or metal filigree.

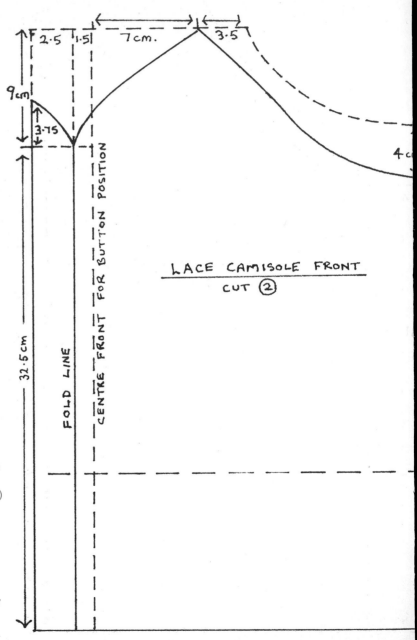

LACE CAMISOLE FRONT
CUT ②

Lace Camisole Top

Inclusive of 1·5cm side seams.
5mm all other seams

1, 2

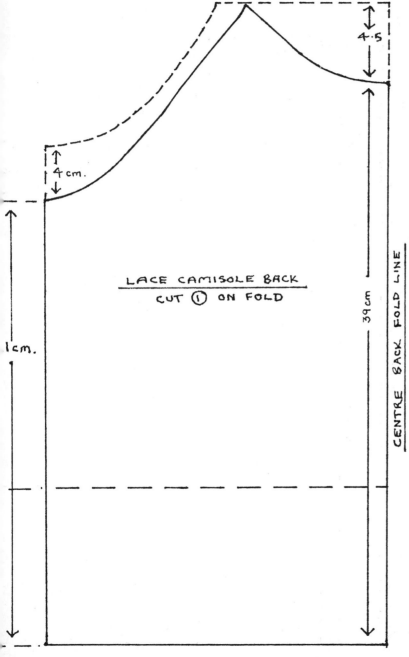

LACE CAMISOLE BACK
CUT ① ON FOLD

4·5

4 cm.

1 cm.

39cm

CENTRE BACK FOLD LINE

7 Cut shoulder straps of narrow lace 25cm (10ins) long and pin in position. (If the lace is very fine, topstitch cotton tape underneath to strengthen.)

8 Topstitch fine lace edging (frilled or flat) around every edge, including down the front.

9 Thread narrow elastic that measures 10cm (4ins) shorter than the actual waist measurement. Thread through the taped channel and secure at the centre front.

10 If the fabric is firm enough, buttonhole the front but to avoid any tearing of the lace, it might be advisable to sew the buttons* onto the outside and use small press studs for the fastening.

NB If it is not possible to buy exactly matching lace for the edges, the simplest solution is to buy the lace white and dye it using a ready mixed bought dye.

Diagrams for construction notes 3–10 are as for notes 2–8 for the Shaped Camisole Top With Shoulder Straps

Shaped top camisole with straps

Lace button front camisole

Victorian-Style Camisole

To fit size 12 but, having tucks in the front, it should be quite adaptable in size. If a wider fit is required the side seams can be extended as instructed for camisole no. 2. If made full length it can be converted to make a very attractive nightdress, summer dress or evening dress.

Suggested fabrics:
Broderie anglaise, fine lawn, striped Swiss voile.

Construction details:
Machine needle: size 9 or 11
Thread: mercerized cotton, size 50

1   Draw out the pattern shape as for camisole no. 2, using the same proportions and measurements.
2   Draw in new square armhole and add button wrap on centre back (the centre front now being on the fold).
3   Trace out guide line 5cm (2ins) away from, and parallel to, the top edge. This will be the guide line for topstitching down the wide lace or broderie anglaise trim.
4   Cut out the three pattern pieces, mark the stitching lines for the tucks and machine them from top to bottom, pressing away from the centre front towards the side seams. (If a fuller effect is desired they need only be stitched down to the depth of the lace yoke, i.e. 11cm (4 1/4 ins) from the top.)
6   For a more elaborate effect very fine lace edging can be stitched along the edge of each tuck.
7   Fold in the button wrap at the back and topstitch down.
8   Stitch the side seams ending with 5mm (1/4 in) French seams.

9 Press 5mm (¼in) seam allowance onto the right side, right along the top edge and the hem.

10 Topstitch narrow lace edging on top of the hem hiding the raw edge.

11 Cut two 30cm (20ins) shoulder straps out of the wide broderie anglaise or wide Guipure lace. If there are holes available for insertion thread ribbon through finishing with a bow on the shoulder.

12 Cut one 12cm (5ins) band and treat as above, placing it across the top of the front over the tucks and top stitch down (see diagram).

13 Repeat for the back, using two 8cm (3ins) bands.

14 Topstitch two 30cm (12in) bands (as in stage 11) across the base of the armholes.

15 The shoulder straps can now be attached, topstitching on to bodice, covering the edges of the front and back across bands and mitreing the corner but turning under when it reaches the armhole band (see diagram).

16 Zigzag buttonholes down the back and sew on buttons.

This camisole can be left loose or elasticated around waistline by sewing a channel of tape on the inside and threading elastic through.

Victorian Style Camisole
Inclusive of 1·5cm side seams
5mm all other seams

1, 2, 3

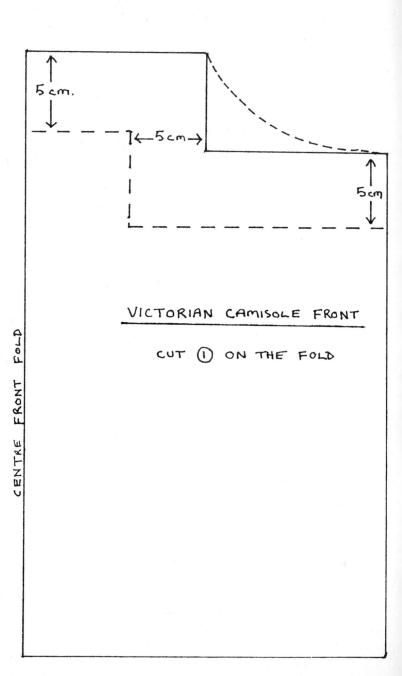

VICTORIAN CAMISOLE FRONT

CUT ① ON THE FOLD

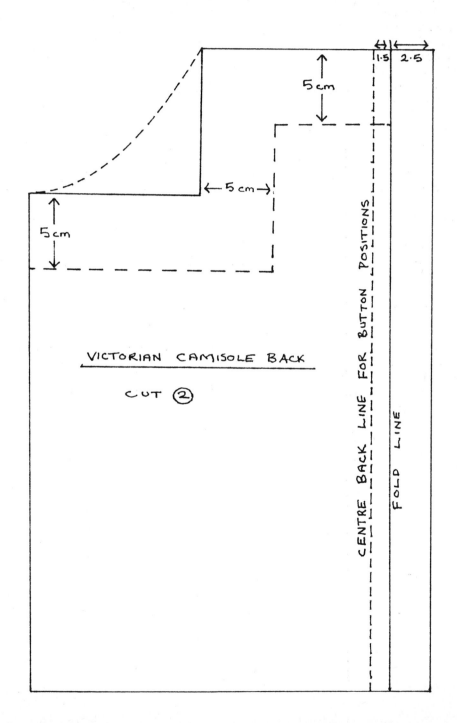

5 cm

5 cm

5 cm

1·5 2·5

CENTRE BACK LINE FOR BUTTON POSITIONS

FOLD LINE

VICTORIAN CAMISOLE BACK

CUT ②

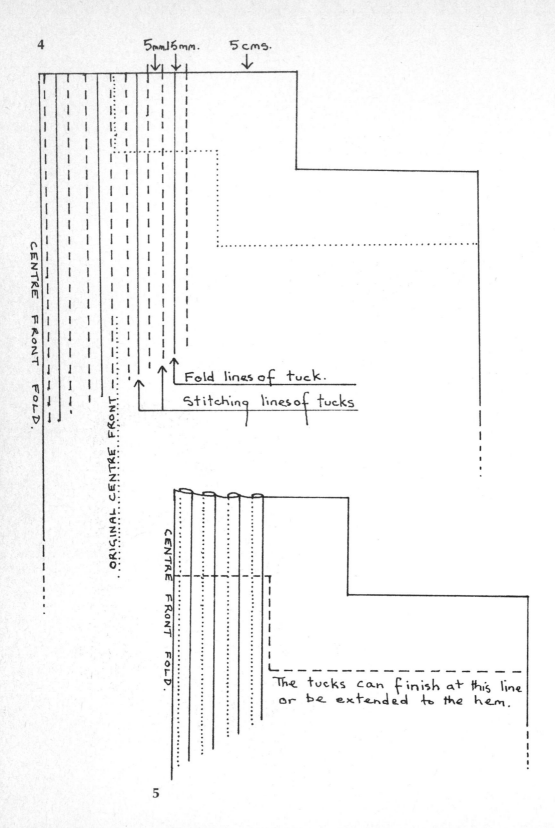

4

5mm 15mm. 5 cms.

CENTRE FRONT FOLD.

ORIGINAL CENTRE FRONT

Fold lines of tuck.
Stitching lines of tucks

CENTRE FRONT FOLD.

The tucks can finish at this line
or be extended to the hem.

5

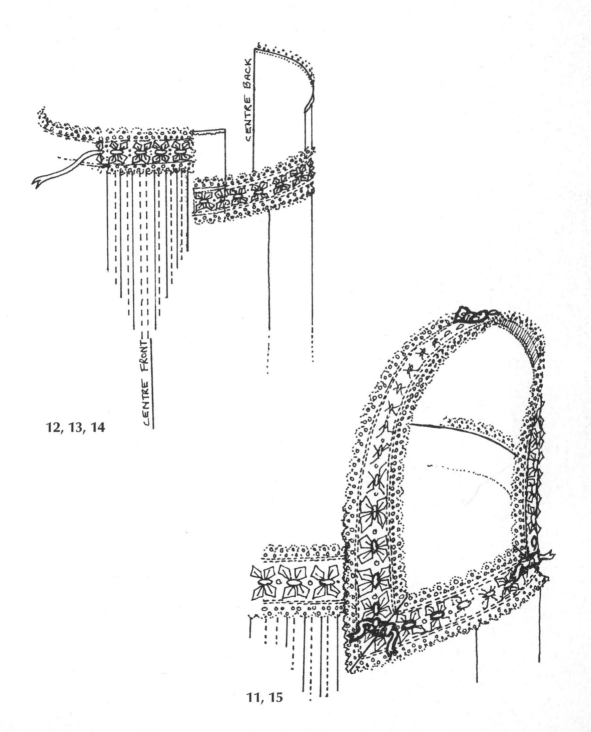

CENTRE BACK

CENTRE FRONT

12, 13, 14

11, 15

FRENCH KNICKERS

The basic construction for the French Knicker uses a size 12 skirt block as for four panel waist slip. Because this shape is elasticated and, therefore, quite loose it is nevertheless adaptable to larger and smaller sizes without changing the pattern.

Suggested fabrics:
Cotton lawn, Swiss voile, satin, silk, crêpe de Chine, Japanese silk.

Construction details:
Machine needle: sizes 9 or 11
Thread: mercerized cotton, size 50 or pure silk thread.
Seams: should be 5mm (¼in) French seams on side seams, front and back seams, inside leg.

1   Draw around front and back skirt block to a depth of 34cm (13½in) on centre front, centre back lines. Although the darts are drawn in, these should be ignored since their fullness will provide extra ease for elastication around the waist.
2   Measure down the centre front and centre back 28cm (11¼in) to point A and B, then draw in a dotted construction line at right angles to these lines CD.
3   From point A measure 7cm (2¾in) away from centre front to mark point E.
4   Repeat from point B and mark point F 11cm (4½in) away from the centre back.
5   From points E and F drop perpendicular lines of 6cm (2½in) to meet the hem line at G and H. Rule a line across.
6   Draw in the seat seams from I to E and J and F by gently curving down from the top to a deeper angle at the crutch.

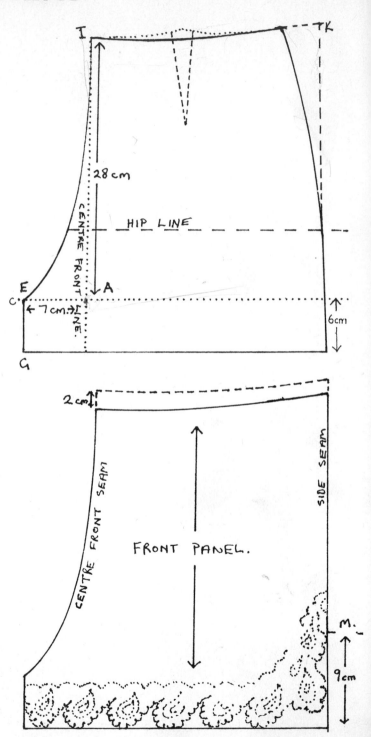

French Knickers

Size 12. To fit 64cm–76cm Waist
88cm–102cm Hip
Drawings to ¼ scale
No's 1–8

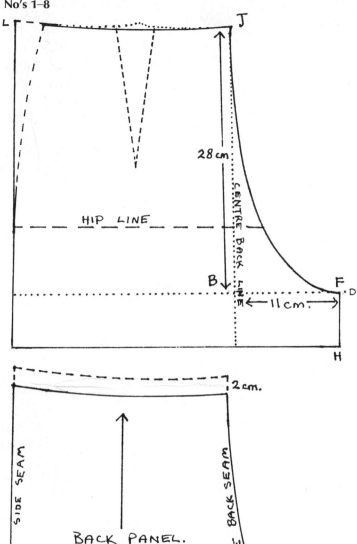

7 Where the side seams are vertical at the hem, continue them upwards in a straight line to points K and L. This will provide more freedom at the waist for elastication.

8 Connect points I to K and L to J with a gentle curve.

9 Trace off the new shapes adding 2cm (¾in) to the waist to provide a self channel for the elastic to be threaded through.

10 Cut out the four pattern pieces, i.e. two front pieces and two back pieces.

11 Sew up the side seams with a 5mm (¼in) French seam, finishing at point M if a 9cm (3½in) slit is desired.

12 If the latter effect is required the opening on the side seam can be left rectangular or turned into a curve.

13 Whichever style is preferred, the following procedure should be adopted: press onto the outside a 5mm (¼in) seam allowance over which lace edging can be topstitched. If a 'see-through' effect is desired the lace should be layed flush with the fabric so both hem edges are aligned. Then the inside edge of the lace should be followed with a tiny zigzag stitch. The fabric underneath the lace can then be cut away right up to the stitching line.

14 Stitch the inside leg seams EG–FH with 5mm (¼in) French seams.

15 Stitch the seat seam from I–E–F–J with a 5mm (¼in) French seam.

16 Press in the waistline for 5mm and then fold over again for 1·5cm (¾in) on to the inside of the garment.

17 Edge stitch down leaving a 1cm (½in) gap at one side seam to provide a channel for the elastic.

18 Thread 5mm (¼in) elastic, cut 10cm (4ins) short of the required waist measurement, through the channel and stitch both ends together so that the waist is now elasticated.

French knickers

Camiknickers

CAMIKNICKERS

Camiknickers, a neat combination of slip and French knickers, were originally popular in the 1920s when worn under the new, clinging bias-cut tubes of dresses. Their revival recently could be explained by their practical simplicity combined with maximum femininity which echoes the general fashion trends of today. The construction of the pattern is relatively simple by adding the top half of the basic full slip to the French knicker pattern.

Camiknickers sewn up for all but one side seam to show leg openings.

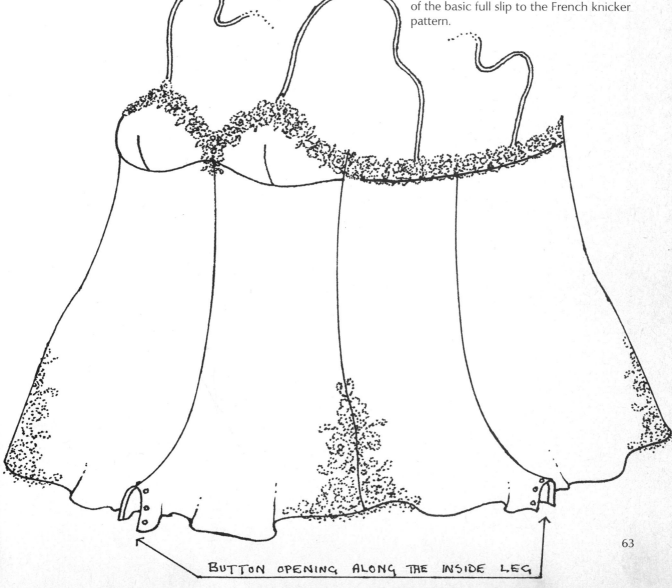

BUTTON OPENING ALONG THE INSIDE LEG

Diagram to size 12. For larger sizes extend the side seams and also the length of the garment by cutting through the waistline and opening up to the required length.

Suggested fabrics:
Silk, crêpe de Chine, Japanese silk, Satin.

Construction details:
Machine needle: sizes 9 or 11
Thread: pure silk thread
For an easier fit and a more attractive hang of the fabric it is suggested that the fabric is cut on the bias. Side seams, centre front and centre back seams 5mm (¼in) French seams.

1 Draw around the front and back patterns of the French knicker pattern.
2 Draw in the centre front and centre back lines at right angles to the hem, passing through points A and B.
3 Measure up from point A for 14cm (5¾in) to point C and then lay the top of the pattern for the front basic full slip. Draw around this curving the side seam to join the knicker side seam at point E which is 20cm (8in) up from the hem line.
4 Repeat this procedure for the back making point D 13cm (5¼in) up the centre back from point B.
5 Add a 2cm (¾in) button wrap at each inside leg, points F and G, for the crutch opening.
6 The bra shape stays the same as for the basic slip.
7 Having cut out the five pattern pieces, firstly sew up the bust darts, trim down to 5mm (¼in) and zigzag the two edges together.
8 Fold in half the four button wraps and topstitch down.
9 Stitch the centre front seam with a 5mm (¼in) French seam.
10 Repeat for the back seam. However, if an opening is required a 2cm (¾in) button wrap should be added along the centre back down to the waistline.
11 Sew bra section to front panels with 1cm (½in) seam. Trim to 5mm (¼in) and zigzag two edges together.

Camiknicker construction using top half of basic full slip added to the French Knicker pattern
Diagram to ¼ scale. Size 12.

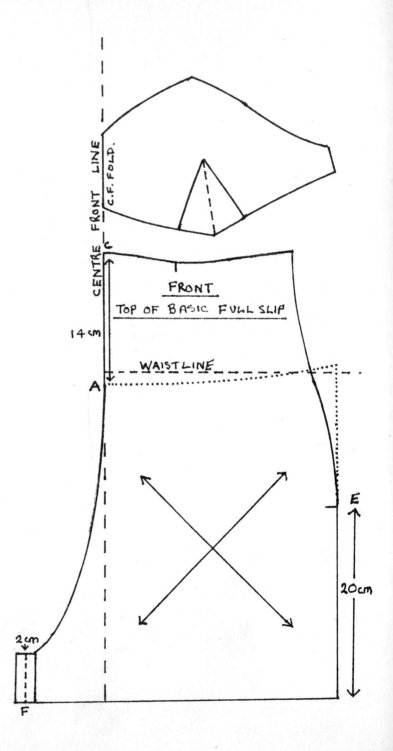

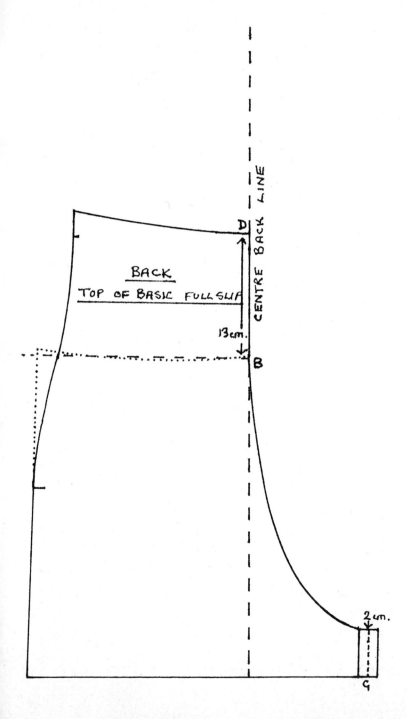

BACK

TOP OF BASIC FULL SLIP

CENTRE BACK LINE

D

13 cm.

B

2 cm.

C

12 Stitch the side seams with 5mm (¼in) French seams.

13 Add narrow satin or 5mm (¼in) rouleau shoulder straps to the required measurement, having pressed on to the outside a 5mm (¼in) seam allowance right the way round the top edge.

14 Zigzag down wide lace edging all the way around the top edge. Do this with the outer edge of the lace just pointing up above the edge of the fabric.

15 Machine a minute hem round the bottom (5mm (¼in) in depth).

16 Lace can then be put all round the hem, or separate motifs cut out to form a triangular shape on the side seams (see diagram)

17 Sew small press studs on to the button wrap.

STRAPLESS CORSELETTE

This garment reached its peak in the Victorian and Edwardian eras yet recently has enjoyed a revival, not only as a provocative undergarment, but as high fashion evening wear. Therefore, if interpreted into more exotic and heavier fabrics such as velvet or brocade, there is no reason why it should not be worn as the barest of evening tops over long full skirts.

Diagrams for size 12. If a larger size is required the waist darts should be decreased and the side seams increased.

Suggested fabrics:
Satin, stretch satin (for a perfect tight fit), brocade, taffeta, velvet.

Construction details:
Needle: size 14
Thread: mercerized cotton, size 40 or pure silk.
Since most of the fabrics are too heavy for French seams, either open seams of 1cm (½in) allowance with zigzagged edges or the seams can be trimmed to 5mm (¼in) and the two raw edges zigzagged together. To avoid the impracticability of opening the front each time it is advisable to use a light weight open ended zip down the centre back. For support and strength of line boning should be inserted down each seam.

1   Using the pattern pieces for the shaped seven panel slip trace off the panels down to the hip line.
2   Add the 4cm (1¾in) point on the centre front line as for the slip with gathered top and deep side slits.
3   To give the waist a tighter fit mark 2cm (¾in) inside the side seam along the waistline and draw in the new side seam as shown by the dotted line.

4 From the waistline at the centre front draw in the new curved front edging down to the hem line.

5 Using the bra cup pattern from the flared slip with lace top cut away the 4cm (1¾in) base to fit into the point of the body panels.

6 Measure down from the point of the bra 4cm (1¾in) and draw in the new lower curve.

7 Repeat stage 3 at the waistline on the back panel.

8 Drop down 3cm (1¼in) from top of centre back line and draw in the curve from the top of the side seam to lower the back line.

9 Add 2cm (¾in) seam allowance down the centre back for the zip.

10 Curve off the hem lines of the separate panels to give a gentle curve all around the hem line.

11 Retrace out the separate panels marking the grain lines and also mark the positions of the eyelets for the ribbon laced front.

12 Having cut out the separate pattern pieces in fabric insert the open ended zip into the centre back seam.

13 Stitch the dart in the bra cup and zigzag the 5mm (¼in) seam allowance. If the fabric is not firm enough to support the bust either stiffen with iron-on stiffening or insert a pair of bought bra cup shapes. For added shape a padded foam cup can be inserted.

14 Press on to the outside a 5mm (¼in) seam around the top edge of the cup. Add a lace frilled edging and then emphasize with narrow satin ribbon (in the case of evening wear, narrow gold or silver Russia braid is most effective).

15 Sew all the panels together treating the seams as mentioned in the construction details. *Leave the centre front open.*

16 Sew the bra cups on to the front sections with the seam allowances on the right side, pressing a 5mm (¼in) seam out on to the outside along the top of the back sections

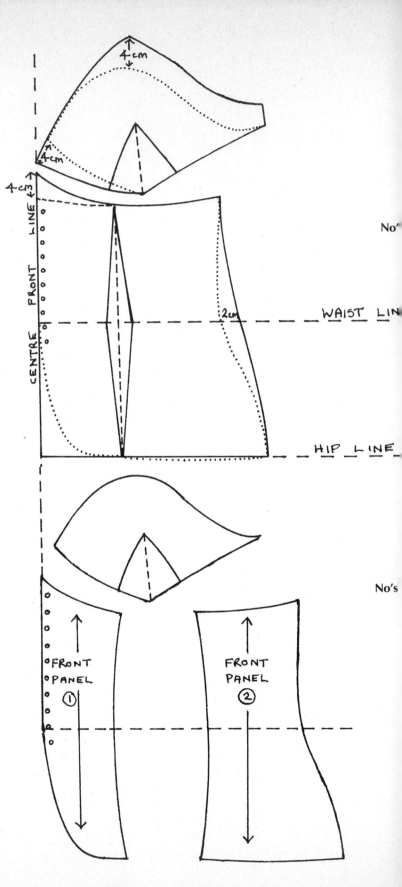

Strapless Corselette

Construction using Bra shape from
the flared slip pattern/bodice from shaped
seven panel slip. Size 12. Drawn to ¼ scale.

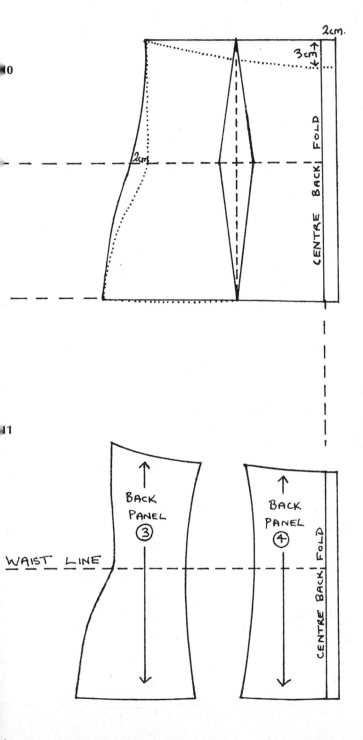

17 Cover these open seams with topstitched narrow satin ribbon or braid.
18 Topstitch channels of lace edged
narrow ribbon down all these seams
starting from the point of the dart in the
case of the front seam.
19 Carefully slide narrow boning up all
these seams underneath the ribbon
channels.
20 Press on to the outside a 5mm (¼ in)
seam down the centre front and around
the hem.
21 Topstitch narrow lace frilled edging
on to this to cover the raw edge.
22 Topstitch a narrow ribbon channel
on the edge of the centre front down to
just below the waistline. Stiffen this with
boning as before.
23 Insert eyelets (these kits can be
bought in good department stores) in the
positions marked on the pattern.
24 Lace up the front in a criss-cross
fashion with satin ribbon.
25 Finally, finish off all the ends of the
boned seams with tiny satin bows (see
illustration).

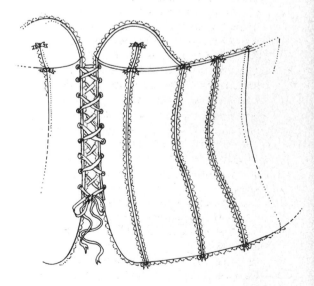

Strapless Corselette
Showing distribution of
ribbon and lace trimming
and centre front fastening

NIGHTDRESS

This chapter starts with a simple 'smock' style nightdress and progresses to elaborate tucked and frilled 'Victorian' style nightdresses. According to the fabric used, how elaborate the trimmings and the length they could equally well be worn as summer dresses or extravagant evening dresses. If a very sensuous and clinging look is desired one only has to utilize the chapter dealing with full slips, i.e. all the slips described can be extended to floor length to create nightdresses that have a maximum effect for a minimum of cut and construction. In all cases when making the slip full length, extend the side seams down to the hem line along the centre back and centre front lines to the desired length. Make sure that the hem curves in a parallel fashion to the original hem of the slip. Obviously, if the side slits are incorporated they can be made much deeper, right up to the hipline or even the waistline. Also, in the case of the nightdresses, the lace trimming can be more extravagant in order to create a lavish look, or deep lace-edged frills can be added as instructed in stage 43 (p. 79) of the Nightdress with Lace Edged Cutouts. As with most of these garments, fine silk, silk crêpe de Chine or satin would be the most suitable to provide the ultimate in luxury and appeal.

Gathered smock nightdress

Simple Smock Nightdress

This versatile nightdress can be made up to any lenght from baby doll to floor length. The 'maximum effect for minimum effort', utilizing the simplest of ingredients, very easily produces an attractive garment. There is no reason why, if worn with a tie belt, it should not make a pretty summer dress. The body is simply gathered up at the top, the edge bound and a decorative applique applied on to the top. The appliques can vary from purchased embroidered motifs, appliqued lace or even those flat, usually linen, coloured flowers found embroidered on to old crochet table mats! Having decorated the smock accordingly, the armhole is bound with a narrow rouleau to form shoulder straps, then trimmed with a frill of the same fabric or a purchased lace frill.

Diagram size 12 but suitable for many sizes since there are ample gathers and no sleeves.

Suggested fabrics:
Broderie anglaise, striped Swiss voile, printed cotton lawn, satin, silk, crêpe de Chine.

Construction details:
Machine needle: according to fineness of fabric sizes 9, 11, 14.
Thread: mercerized cotton size 50 or pure silk
The two side seams can be 5mm (¼ in) French seams or zigzagged double raw edges trimmed to 5mm (¼ in). The neck edges and armholes are bound with a bias cut strip. The applique can be put on by a small machine zigzag or by hand. The frill on the armhole can be repeated on the hem but this is purely optional.

Nightdress, cut away shoulder and neck

1 Draw around the front and back blocks, ignoring the darts extending from the sides down to the waistline.

2 Measure down the centre front 15cm (6in) and mark point A.

3 Measure a further 2cm (¾in) down and mark point B.

4 Measure 4cm (1¾in) centres down from armhole C to D and rule a construction line across to B.

5 From line DB measure up for 10cm (4in) at right angles to this line and mark point on the armhole.

6 Repeat these five procedures for the back block marking points C, D, E, F, G.

7 Divide each block into sections by measuring along the construction lines DB and FD at three, 4cm (1¾in) points away from centre front and centre back.

8 Rule vertical lines through these points down to the hem to give sections 1, 2, 3 and 4.

9 Cut away the top curved sections of the block since this will not be needed.

10 The side seams, centre front and centre back can now be extended to the length required, e.g. baby doll, knee length, calf length or floor length.

11 Cut the back and front patterns into four sections down the dotted construction lines.

12 Rule a fresh line on the paper 80cm (32in) long (D to D) to use as a construction line when adding the fullness for the gathers.

Smock Nightdress, Short or Long Gathered onto Embroidered Yoke and Frills on Shoulder Straps
No seams included

No's 1–8

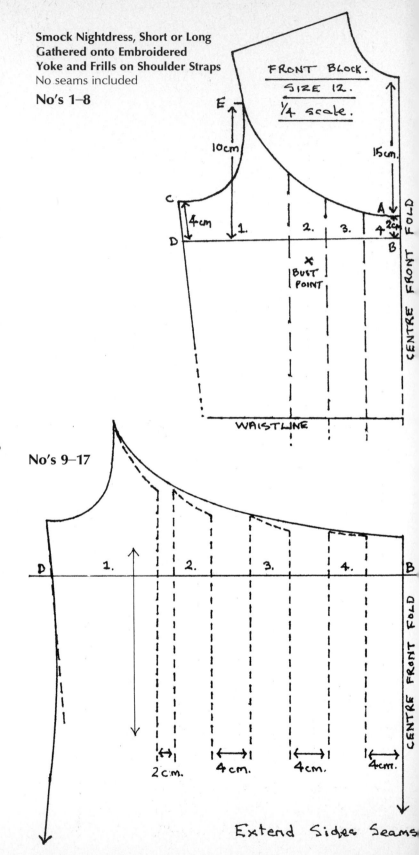

FRONT BLOCK.
SIZE 12.
¼ scale.

No's 9–17

Extend Sides Seams

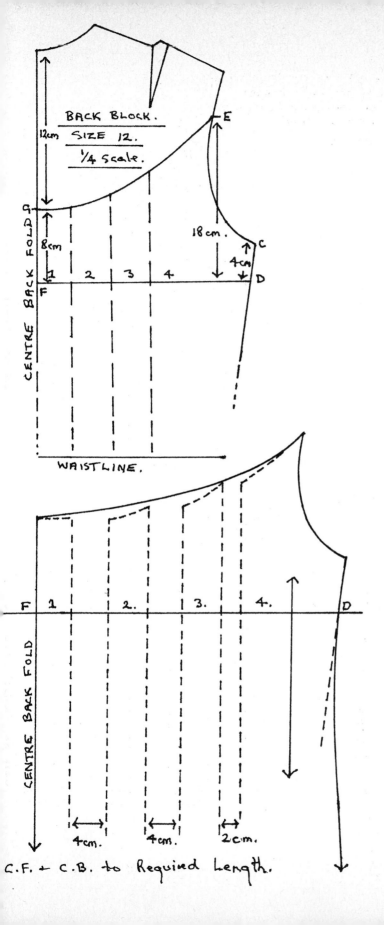

BACK BLOCK.
SIZE 12.
1/4 scale.

12cm

9cm

E

CENTRE BACK FOLD

8cm

18 cm.

C

4cm

1 2 3 4 D

F

WAISTLINE.

F 1 2. 3. 4. D

CENTRE BACK FOLD

4cm. 4cm. 2cm.

C.F. + C.B. to Required Length.

13　Lay the cut sections along this line so that lines DB and FD are on top of the 80cm (32in) DD line.

14　Starting at front side seam, affix panel 1 in place then panel 2 placed 2cm (¾in) away from panel 1 along line DD.

15　Panels 3 and 4 are placed at 4cm (1¾in) intervals and a further 4cm (1¾in) is added to the centre front.

16　Repeat for the back panel but do not add 4cm (1¾in) on centre back.

17　Draw around the new pattern shapes.

18　Cut out the two panels on the fold of the fabric.

19　Run a double gathering thread 1cm (½in) in from the top edges and gather the front up to 24cm (9½in) and the back up to 20cm (8in). (Make sure that the fullness is deepest at the centre fronts and centre backs.)

20　Bind these two edges with a bias cut strip cut 4cm (1¾in) wide so that the finished edge is 1cm (½in) (the method is the same as the basic bra in the first chapter).

21　The chosen decoration can now be applied to the top edge of the front so that it overlaps the edge, consequently hiding the binding.

22 Cut two 96cm (38½in) strips of the fabric 5cm (2in) wide for the frills on the armhole. (These do not necessarily have to be in the same fabric as the nightdress. Ready bought lace frills would be just as effective.)

23 Cut four 48in (19in) bias strips 2cm (¾in) wide (these can be made larger if wished by measuring around the person's armhole loosely) for the armhole straps.

24 Join the strips into four circles pressing one seam allowance in of 5mm (¼in) around one edge of each circle.

25 Pin one raw edge of the strip on to the outside of the armhole with the pressed seam allowance pointing outwards.

26 Repeat this procedure on the inside of the armhole with the other strip so that there are three thicknesses of fabric.

27 Once past the armhole, pin the rest of the two strips together, right sides together, to form a complete circle.

28 Machine around 5mm (¼in) in and press both strips away from the garment towards the armhole. The two folded edges should now meet with both seam allowances hidden on the inside.

29 Insert the frill between the two circular strips and topstitch the edge, right the way through all the layers, to seal off all raw edges and complete the shoulder straps and armhole binding all in one.

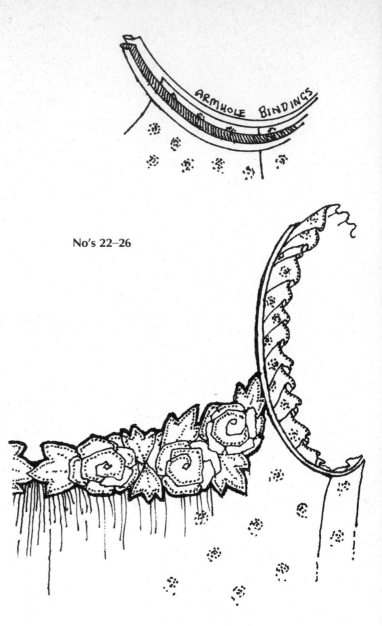

No's 22–26

Nightdress with Cutouts

This is an equally adaptable garment due to the fact that if interpreted in practical cotton, it could easily make a pretty summer dress, short or long. But if produced in a more luxurious fabric such as silk, the garment with its cutaway shoulders and front could be exotic and provocative as a nightdress or evening dress.

Size 12 but easily adapted to larger sizes by extending the side seams. The tie neck and shoulder plus gathered front give plenty of ease.

Suggested fabrics:
Broderie anglaise, printed cotton lawn, Swiss voile, satin, silk.

Construction details:
Needles: machine needle size 9 or 11
Thread: mercerized cotton, no. 50 or pure silk
5mm (¼in) seams for the sides and armholes. Otherwise all edges are bound with a bias strip or ribbon.

1 Draw around front bodice block size 12 (only as far as waist).
2 Measure 2cm (¾in) away from shoulder point A to give point B. Curve the new cut away armhole down to the single balance notch (see diagram).
3 Mark 2cm (¾in) down centre front from C and mark point D.
4 Join B and D with a shallow curve for the new neck line.
5 Measure down the centre front from point D 10cm (4in) to E. (This can be lowered by 5cm (2in) for a more daring effect!)
6 Draw in the curved cut away sections as on diagram.

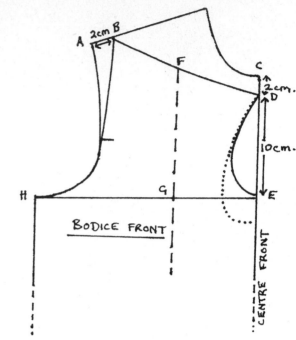

No's 1–8

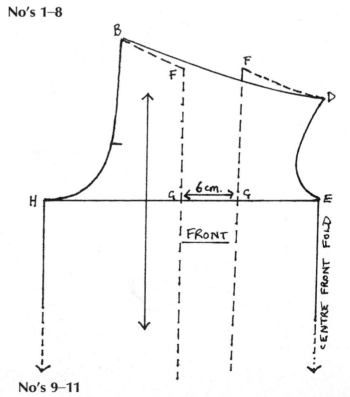

No's 9–11

Nightdress with lace edged cutouts
Size 12. ¼ scale
No seams

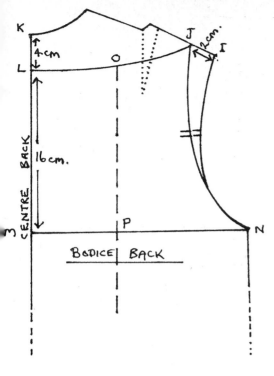

No's 12–18

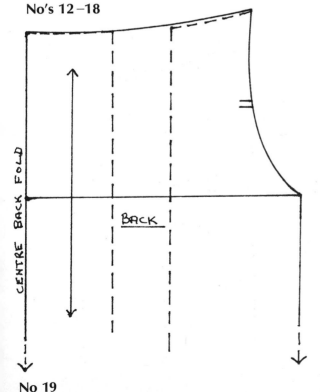

No 19

7   Measure half way along new shoulder line BD and mark F.

8   From F drop a straight line, parallel to the centre front line to cross the construction line HE at G.

9   Cut out the pattern having extended the side seam and centre front line to the required length.

10   Cut through line FG down to the hem and keeping line HE level, space the two pieces apart for 6cm (2½in). This provides the fullness in the front.

11   Join points B and D with a gentle curve.

12   Draw around the back bodice block down to the waist.

13   As for the front measure 2cm (¾in) away from I on the shoulder point and mark point J. Curve down from point J into original armhole.

14   Measure down the centre back from K 4cm (1¾in) to point L.

15   Join L and J with a shallow curve to produce the new back neckline (disregard the shoulder dart).

16   Measure 16cm (6½in) from L to M and connect with the underarm point N to give the construction line MN.

17   Measure half way between L and J to give point O.

18   Drop a straight line parallel to the centre back to cross line MN at P.

19   Repeat procedures 9–11 for lengthening the back and adding the fullness.

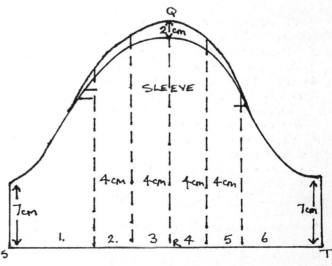

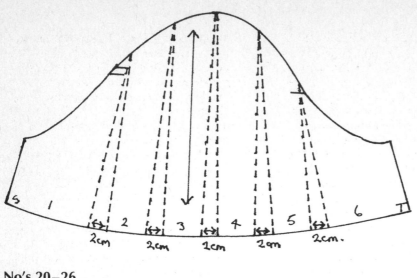

No's 20–26

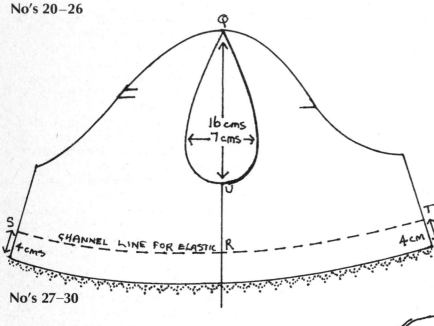

16 cms
← 7 cms →

CHANNEL LINE FOR ELASTIC R

4cm

No's 27–30

20 Draw around the sleeve block to a seam length 7cm (2¾in)
21 Raise the sleeve head 2cm (¾in) curving down to the balance notches at either side (this compensates the 2cm (¾in) which have been taken away from the shoulder on the bodice). Point Q.
22 Drop a central guide line down from Q to the hem line ST to give point R.
23 Mark two parallel lines either side of QR line all 4cm (1¾in) apart.
24 Cut out the pattern and cut through the dotted lines from the bottom up to the sleeve head, but not right through.

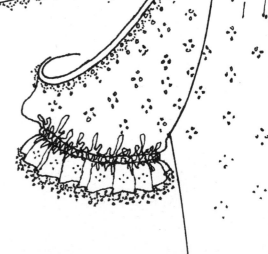

No's 31–43

25 To add the flare to the sleeve, starting from the central line QR, open up the sections of the sleeve so that each has a gap of 2cm (¾ in) between them, tapering to nothing at the top.

26 Join up the bottom sections with a gentle curve to form the new hem.

27 Trace off the new shape sleeve pattern, adding 4cm (1¾ in) on to the hem for the frill.

28 Measure 16cm (6½ in) down line QR to give point U.

29 Measure across QU, 9cm (3½ in) down and 7cm (2¾ in) across.

30 Using these measurements as a guide, sketch in the cut away shape.

31 Cut out the four pieces of the nightdress to the length you require (front/back on fold, sleeves × 2).

32 Bind the front opening using a folded 3cm (1¼ in) bias strip (possibly in a contrast fabric or bias satin ribbon) as for the instructions for bikini bra on p. 14. Sandwich lace or broderie anglaise frills inside while doing this.

33 Repeat this procedure for the opening in the sleeve.

34 Topstitch a narrow cotton tape channel for the elastic on the wrong side along line ST. (Remember to finish the tape 2cm (¾ in) away from the side seams.)

35 Press a 5mm (¼ in) seam allowance on to the right side of the sleeve hem.

36 Cover this by topstitching a lace frill over the edge.

37 Sew front and back bodies to sleeve heads with a 5mm (¼ in) French seam matching double notches at back and single notches at the front.

38 Stitch side seams of body and side seams of sleeve with a continuous 5mm (¼ in) French seam.

39 Run two lines of gathering stitches around front and back of the neck.

40 Draw the back up until it measures 36cm (14½ in) and secure.

41 Repeat for the front so that each half measures 16cm (6½ in).

42 Bind the neck edges as in stage 32, adding extra 20cm (8in) at each shoulder and the centre front for rouleau ties. (These should be made as for the basic bikini bra see page 14.)

43 The hem can be treated as for stages 35 and 36, but if desired a frill can be added by cutting a straight band of fabric, three times the length of hem, 16cm (6½ in) deep. This should be zigzagged to the hem on the inside and, ideally, lace edged as for the sleeve. This garment can be made to look more elaborate by using a deeper lace frill, adding ribbon bows at the base of the U-shaped cutouts and by the use of exotic fabrics.

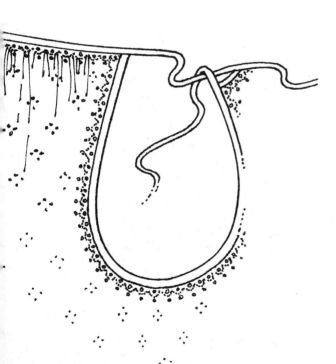

Victorian Nightdress with Pintucks (Stitched Pleats)

This versatile garment can be utilized, according to the fabric, as a nightdress, evening dress, summer dress or shirt. It has a bib front with ribbon ties, pintucked (stitched pleats) bodice and sleeve head, elasticated frilled cuff, stand collar and shirt tail hem. The length can vary from hip length for a shirt, knee length for a dress and full length for a nightdress or evening dress (any length would be suitable for sleep wear)

Size 12, but adaptable to size 14–16–18 since it is a loose cut and can be made larger by opening up the pleats to a wider width.

Suggested fabrics:
Striped Swiss voile, broderie anglaise, printed lawn, striped cotton, Viyella, silk.

Construction details:
Needles: sizes 9, 11, 14 – depending on type of fabric.
Thread: mercerized cotton, size 50 or pure silk thread.
All exposed seams should be 5mm (¼in) French seams. All other edges are either enclosed or pressed on to the outside and covered with topstitched lace edging.

1 Draw around the front block down to waist level.
2 To make the armhole larger and looser extend the shoulder 2·5cm (1in) at A and drop the armhole 3·5cm (1½in).
3 Draw in the new shallower curve as in the diagram. Mark armhole notch to match front of sleeve.

4 Mark point C 3·5cm (1½in) in from the neck along the shoulder line.

5 Measure down the centre front for 24cm (9½in) to point D and draw in the shape of the bib front. Cut out and add 1cm (½in) seams on all edges.

6 Measure 16cm (6½in) down from C to F and draw in construction line GF at right angles to CF.

7 From F along this line mark four dotted lines, parallel to CF and 2cm (¾in) between each one.

8 Extend these lines down to the hem line.

9 Cut out the pattern and also through the dotted lines to divide it into five separate pieces.

10 Draw construction GF extended for 20cm (8in).

11 Place pattern pieces along this line so that the two GFs correspond, but with 1·5cm (⅝in) gaps between 1, 2, 3, 4 and 5. This will give the extra depth for the stitched down pleats.

12 Draw in the new shoulder line as shown on the diagram.

13 The dotted lines show the stitching together lines for the four pleats, whilst line GF marks where the stitching should end. Add seam allowances on all edges.

14 Draw round the back block and repeat stages 1–3 to change the armhole.

15 Extend the centre back by 3cm (1¼in) to provide a box pleat with the fold being on the 1·5cm (⅝in) line. Add seam allowances.

16 Draw around the basic sleeve block to a side seam depth of 9·5cm (3¾in), C to B. Rule a line across.

17 Lower the underarm points 3·5cm (1½in), points CA.

18 Lower the crown of the sleeve 2·5cm (1in) from D and sketch in the new sleeve shape.

19 From the centre line D measure three points on either side, all 2·5cm (1in) apart. Rule parallel lines to D from these points up to top of sleeve, dividing the sleeve into seven parts.

20 Having cut along the dotted lines to separate the pieces, draw a new BB construction line 44cm (17¾in) long.

21 Starting with pattern piece no. 1 place all the pieces in numerical order along the line BB with a 1·5cm (⅝in) gap between each one.

22 Draw around the pattern with the top of the pleats as in the diagram.

23 Draw the side seams down to the required length, adding on an extra 8cm (3in) for the frill round the wrist. Add seam allowances on all edges.

24 For the collar draw a rectangle 23cm (9¼in) long by 5cm (2in) deep.

25 Measure 5cm (2in) in from centre front and draw a horizontal line up to top of collar (dotted line).

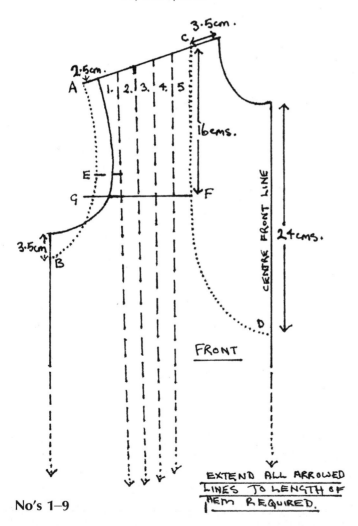

No's 1–9

26 From CF draw a curve up to this line to shape the front of the collar. This will give you the pattern for ½ collar. Add 5mm (¼in) seam allowances.

27 Having cut out all the garment pieces mark the stitching lines for the pleats on the front panel and the sleeves by tacking. (If a striped voile is used this would be much simpler since the guide lines would already be there in the stripe.)

28 Machine up all the pleats but only down as far as lines GF and BB.

29 On the front panel press the pleats away from the centre front and on the sleeves press the pleats towards the centre.

30 The bib front should be *double* so cut 4 pieces.

31 Pin six 20cm (8in) ribbon ties in position down the centre fronts before sewing the two fronts together down the centre front and round the curve. This leaves the shoulder and neck unsewn.

32 Trim and clip the seam allowances of the curve before turning the fabric to right side and pressing the seamed edges. You should now have two double bib panels.

33 To prevent the U-shape on the pleated front panel from stretching, machine a tight row of stitching 5mm (¼in) in from the edge.

34 Slash the seam allowance on the curve and press to the right side of the fabric.

35 Machine a narrow lace frill to the edge of the bib with the two centre fronts edge to edge.

36 Topstitch bib to the front so that it covers the pressed out raw edge.

37 Stitch the shoulder darts on the back panel.

38 Press in the box pleat on centre back and anchor down with a box of topstitching (see diagram).

39 Stitch shoulder seam with a 5mm (¼in) French seam.

40 Take one of the two collar pieces and press to the wrong side a 5mm (¼in) seam allowance along neck edge.

Victorian Nightdress
Stitched pleats on front and sleeves
Bib front with ribbon ties
Size 12. Drawn to ¼ scale
No seams

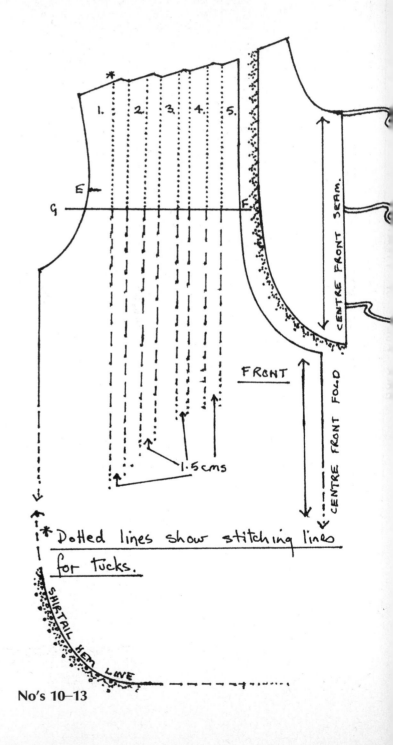

No's 10–13

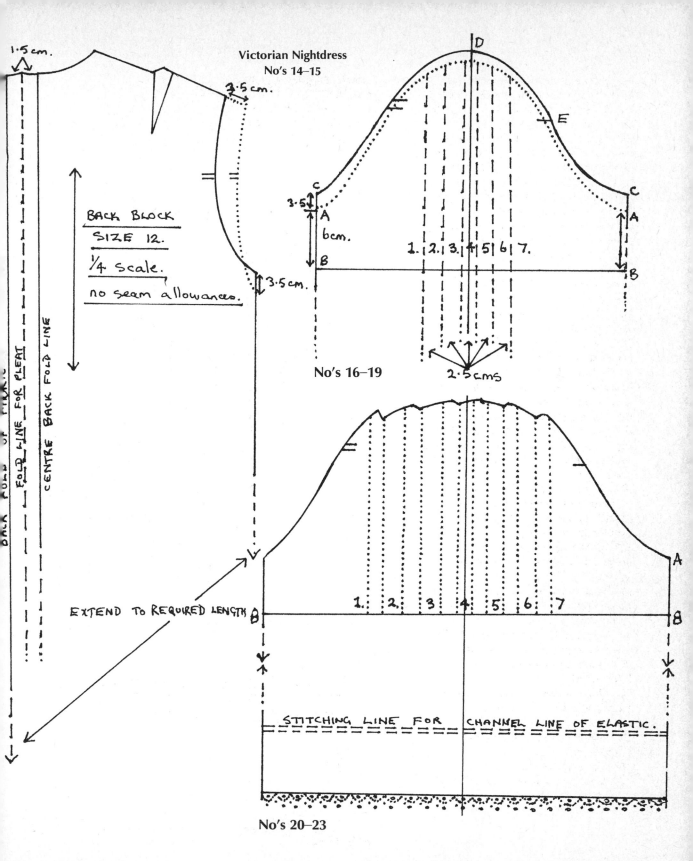

Victorian Nightdress
No's 14–15

1.5 cm.

3.5 cm.

BACK BLOCK
SIZE 12.
¼ scale.
no seam allowances.

3.5 cm.

3.5 cm.

BACK FOLD OF FRAME

FOLD LINE FOR PLEAT

CENTRE BACK FOLD LINE

EXTEND TO REQUIRED LENGTH

D

C

E

C

3.5

A

6cm.

B

A

B

1. 2. 3. 4. 5. 6. 7.

No's 16–19

2.5 cms

A

A

B

B

1.   2.   3   4   5   6   7

STITCHING LINE FOR   CHANNEL LINE OF ELASTIC.

No's 20–23

83

41   Place two collar pieces right sides together and machine around top edge with a 5mm (¼in) seam.

42   Pin the neck edge of the collar, which is not pressed, up to the inside neck of the garment. Machine on with a 5mm (¼in) seam.

45   Clip neck seams and press collar upwards.

46   The pressed edge of the collar can now be topstitched on to the neck of the garment, sandwiching all the seam allowances up inside the collar.

47   Finally, topstitch narrow lace to the outside edge of the collar to match the edge of the bib.

48   Sew the pleated sleeve heads in the armholes using a 5mm (¼in) French seam. Make sure that the double notches match at the back and the single ones at the front.

49   Stitch narrow cotton tape along the wrist line, forming a channel for the elastic. It is important to finish the tape at least 1·5cm (⅝in) away from the side seams so that it does not get sealed when these are stitched.

50   Press a 5mm (¼in) turning around the hem of the sleeve. Topstitch a lace frill to hide this.

51   Pin the side seams and sleeves and machine right the way through using a 5mm (¼in) French seam. Finish this seam at the beginning of the shirt tail slit at the bottom (the length of the slit is entirely up to the individual).

52   Press a 5mm (¼in) seam to the outside all the way around the slit and hem and cover this by topstitching down a narrow lace frill to match the rest.

53   Thread elastic through the channel in the sleeve to create the lace edged wrist frill.

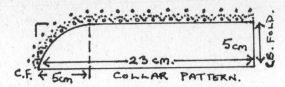

No's 24–26

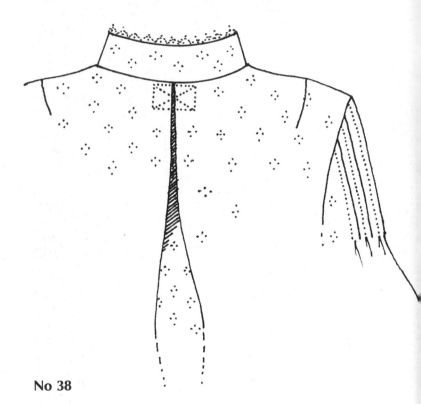

No 38

NEGLIGEES

Negligees, although now less popular than in the past still retain an aura of luxury and sensuality. More recently the practicality of the ubiquitous housecoat seems to have ousted the opulence of the negligee. However, there is no reason why this most delicate and feminine garment cannot be revived and reinstated to the position it held in Victorian times.

Basic Flared Negligee

This is suitable for wearing over any of the lace-edged, full-length slips made as nightdresses (see pages 30–34). This garment has flared sleeves, a deep V-neck and all edges trimmed in deep lace. The front can be edge-to-edge or tied with a deep ribbon sash.
Size 12 but adaptable to larger sizes because of its flare.

Suggested fabrics:
Silk crêpe de Chine, Japanese silk, shantung, cotton voile, satin, broderie anglaise.

Construction details:
Needles: sizes 9 or 11
Thread: silk thread
All seams 5mm (¼ in) French seams. All edges pressed to right side and covered with lace edging.

1 Draw round basic back block down to waistline, ignoring the waist dart.
2 Drop a vertical line down from the underarm point A to 2cm (¾ in) from the waist to straighten the side seam and extend to required hem length.
3 Drop the centre back line down to the required length.
4 Lower the back neck edge 2cm (¾ in) for the lace edging.
5 Divide the remaining shoulder into three 4cm (1¾ in) sections at B and C.
6 Drop lines B and C down to the hem line, parallel to centre back.
7 Draw out front bodice block down to the waist line and straighten out side seam as for back block.
8 Remove shoulder dart by cutting a line through the waist dart up to the bust point and then folding away the shoulder dart. This will automatically open the waist dart and flare out the side seam.

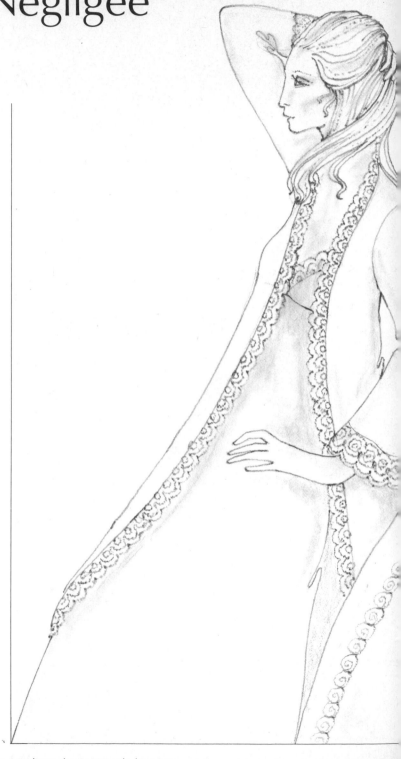

Negligee, basic V neck, lace trim worn over long slip as nightdress

9 Mark 2cm (¾in) in from the neck along the shoulder and draw in V-shaped neck as for Quilted Silk Jacket (see page 103).

10 Divide the remaining shoulder into three 4cm (1¾in) sections at F and G.

11 Drop points F and G down to H and I on the hemline parallel to centre front (extend side seams and centre front to required hem length).

12 Flare out the sleeve exactly as for the Quilted Jacket pattern but add 4cm (1¾in) at each gap in this case.

13 Cut out front and back patterns and cut up lines BD, CE, FH and GI from the hem line up to the shoulder (but not right through the shoulder).

14 Open the bottom sections D, E, H and I to form 8cm (3in) gaps.

15 Draw in the new curved hem line.

16 Straighten out shoulder line since in flaring out the panels it will have curved a little.

17 Cut out pattern pieces in fabric.

18 Stitch shoulder seams using 5mm (¼in) French seams.

19 Stitch sleeve heads into armhole using 5mm (¼in) French seams.

20 Stitch side seams of sleeve and body in one continuous 5mm (¼in) French seam.

21 Press to right side of garment a 5mm (¼in) seam around all edges.

22 Deep lace edging or a lace frill can then be zigzagged to all edges covering the pressed out raw edges.

23 Ribbon ties can be added at the front opening or a sash in matching fabric if desired. Otherwise the garment can be left with an edge to edge opening.

Negligee, lace bodice and sleeves, gathered body

Basic flared negligee
Size 12. Drawn ¼ scale
No seams

No's 1–11

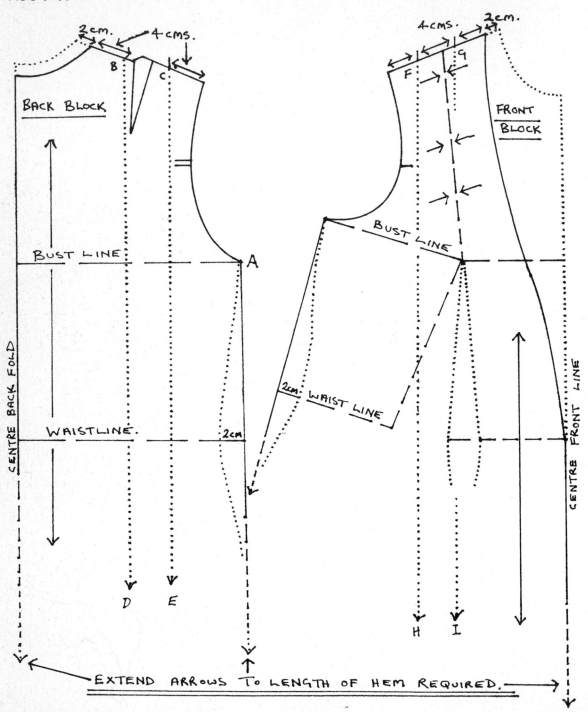

BACK BLOCK

FRONT BLOCK

BUST LINE

WAISTLINE.

CENTRE BACK FOLD

2 cm. 4 cms.

B C

A

2cm

D E

2cm WAIST LINE

BUST LINE

4 cms. 2 cm.

F 9

CENTRE FRONT LINE

H I

EXTEND ARROWS TO LENGTH OF HEM REQUIRED.

Victorian nightdress (see page 80)

Victorian negligée (see page 95)

Unisex sleepsuits (see pages 98-104)

Nightwear into evening wear

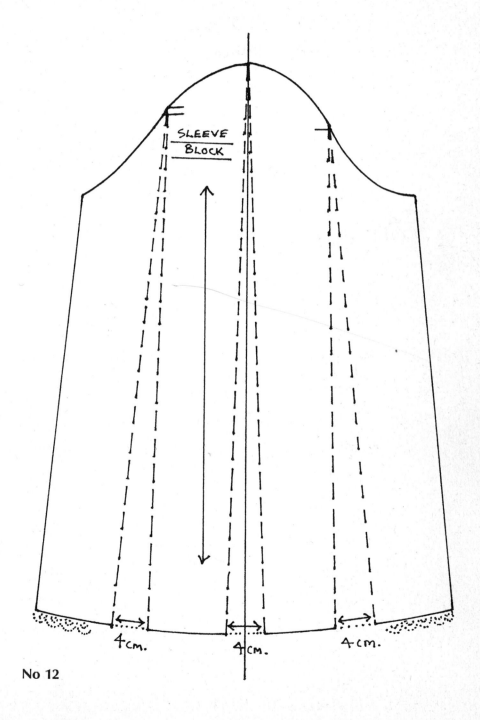

SLEEVE
BLOCK

4 cm.   4 cm.   4 cm.

No 12

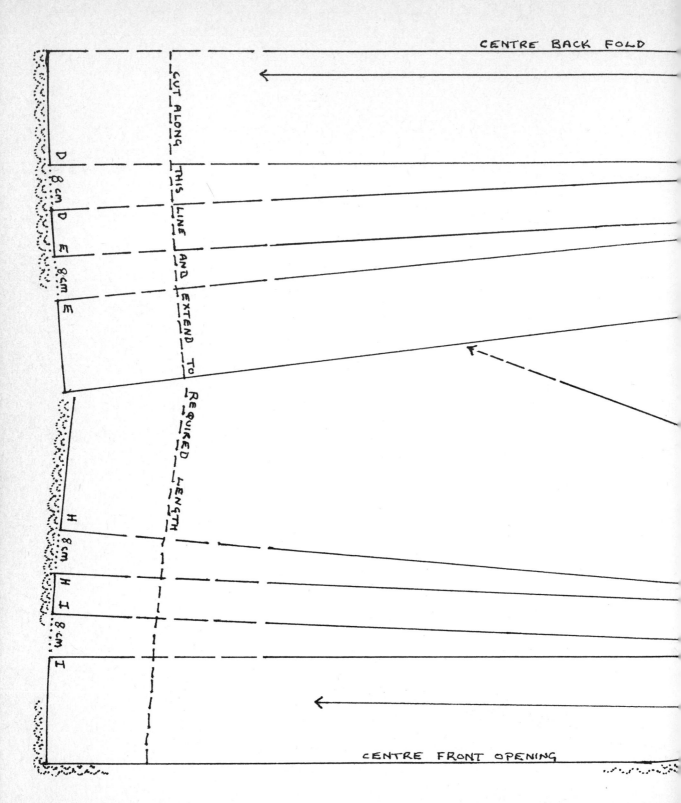

CENTRE BACK FOLD

CUT ALONG THIS LINE AND EXTEND TO REQUIRED LENGTH

D
8 cm
D
E
8 cm
E
H
8 cm
H
I
8 cm
I

CENTRE FRONT OPENING

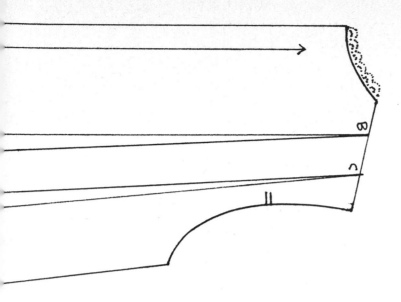

No's 13–16

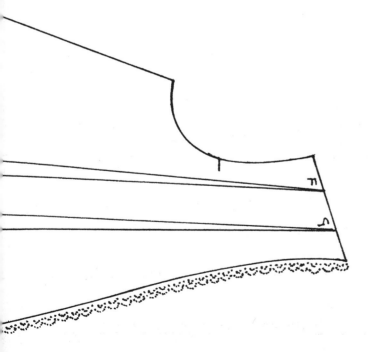

Negligee with lace top and sleeves

This negligee, although of simple construction relies on its lace bodice and, in fact, can be made more elaborate by edging the front hem with lace-edged frills. Similarly, the fabric used can enhance the effect of feminine luxury. It can be made short or long.
Size 12 but adaptable since the body is gathered.

Suggested fabrics:
Silk crêpe de Chine (plain or printed), satin, flowered printed or striped Swiss voile, lace.

Construction details:
Needles: 9 or 11
Thread: pure silk thread
5mm (¼in) French seams for the main body. For seams in the lace, either trim to 5mm (¼in) and zigzag the two raw edges together or bind the edges together with a narrow bias strip cut from the fabric of the garment.

1 Draw around the front and back basic blocks disregarding the darts and extending the side seams, centre front and centre back to the required hem length.
2 Eliminate the back shoulder dart by shortening the shoulder line by the width of the dart and redrawing the armhole (see diagram).

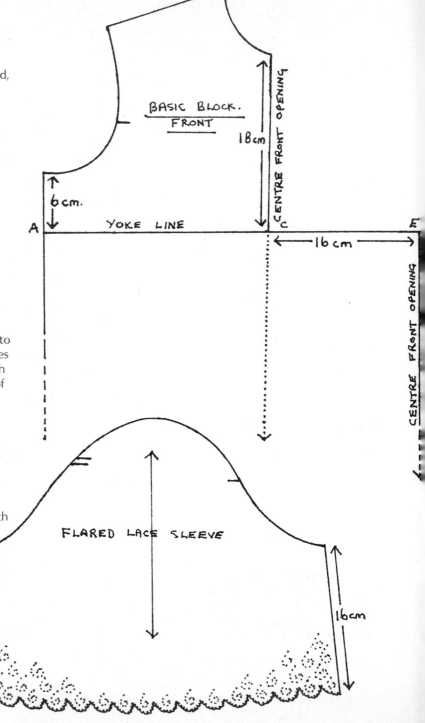

**Negligee with lace top
and sleeves. Gathered body**
Size 12. Drawn to ¼ scale.
No seams

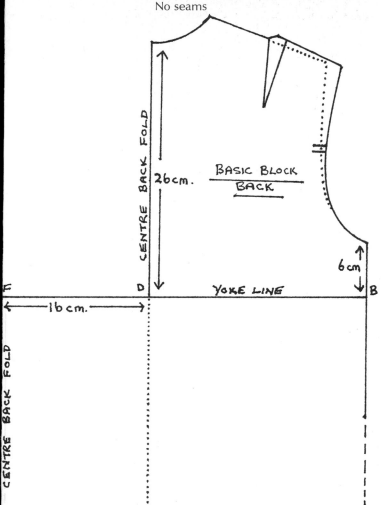

3 Measure down from both armholes 6cm (2½in) for points A and B.
4 Measure 18cm (7in) down centre front to give point C and 26cm (10½in) down centre back to give point D.
5 Rule a line connecting points A–C and D–B to give yoke line.
6 Extend yoke lines for 16cm (6½in) to points E and F and give the gathering allowance. Extend to hem line.
7 Draft out sleeve pattern from Basic Flared Negligee, shortening side seams to 16cm (6½in).
8 The collar is a straight band of lace 32cm (12¾in) long with the top edge cut around the pattern of the lace.
9 Add seam allowances to all patterns before cutting them out.
10 Cut out lace yokes, trimming round the yoke line and centre fronts following the motifs of the lace.
11 Cut out the lace sleeves and treat the hem as above.
12 Stitch side seams of lace yoke either by binding the edges or zigzagging together.
13 Stitch side seams of fabric using 5mm (¼in) French seams.
14 Topstitch lace edging down centre front opening and around hem if wished.
15 Run a double gathering stitch around the top edge of the fabric and gather up to the measurement of the yoke line (92cm (36½in)).
16 Bind the gathered edge with matching coloured seam binding or a bias strip of the same fabric.
17 Place the lace yoke on top of the gathering with the scalloped edge overlapping the bound edge of the fabric.
18 Topstitch down with a zigzag stitch.
19 Stitch shoulder seams binding the seam allowances together with a bias strip of the fabric.

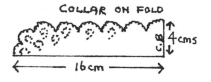

COLLAR ON FOLD

4cms

16cm

20 Stitch side seams of sleeves and zigzag the 5mm (¼ in) seams together.

21 Insert the sleeves and bind the armholes, also with bias strips.

22 Stitch collar on with seam allowances on right side.

23 Cover the seam allowances with topstitched satin ribbon to end in ties at the front.

24 Add four more ribbon ties down the front of the lace yoke.

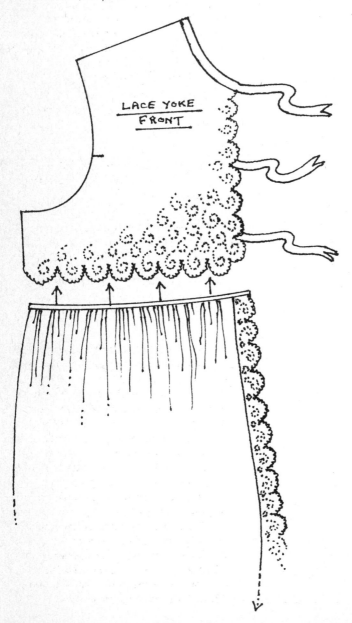

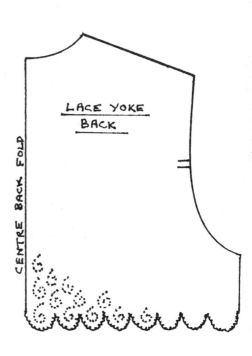

Victorian Style Negligee

This opulent negligee in true Victorian splendour relies entirely on how the basic shape is trimmed with lace, frills and pleated edging. Similarly the fabric used can range from broderie anglaise to the extravagance of the entire garment made in lace. The shape is the same as the Basic Flared Negligee (see pages 88–90) with the addition of a curved yoke. Size 12 but adaptable to larger sizes due to its fullness.

Suggested fabrics:
Broderie anglaise, embroidered Swiss voile, striped voile, silk crêpe de Chine, satin lace.

Construction details:
Needles: size 9 or 11
Thread: mercerized cotton 50, pure silk thread.
5mm (¼in) French seams at sides and shoulder. Armhole zigzagged. All other edges covered in lace.

1 Draw around Flared Negligee pattern (pages 88–90) adding natural neckline of basic bodice block.
2 Mark 8cm (3in) down centre front from neck for starting point of yoke.
3 Mark 10cm (4in) and 12cm (4¾in) points as shown as a guide to draw the curve in for the yoke.
4 Trace off back block for Basic Flared Negligee pattern.
5 Draw in back yoke as shown on diagram on page 97.
6 The sleeve pattern is exactly the same as for Flared Negligee pattern.
7 Cut out pattern pieces adding 1cm (½in) seam allowances on all edges.
8 Stitch shoulder seams of yoke using 5mm (¼in) French seams.

9 Stitch yoke to back and front with the seams on right side.

10 Stitch sleeve head to armhole and zigzag the seams together, trimmed to 5mm (¼ in) on the inside.

11 Topstitch ribbon threaded broderie anglaise or lace frilling down the middle of the two fronts and down the back where marked.

12 Topstitch the same trimming around the yoke, covering the yoke seam allowances and tops of the downward frills.

13 Stitch the side seams of the sleeves and body in one continuous 5mm (¼ in) French seam.

14 Stitch ready bought pleated edging or lace frilling around the hem with seam allowances on the right side.

15 Cover the seam allowance by stitching ribbon threaded broderie anglaise all the way round the top of the frill or pleating.

16 Press centre front seam allowance to right side and topstitch the edging used in stage 15 down the front.

17 Repeat stages 14 and 15 for the cuff to which the sleeve is gathered.

18 Trim with ribbon bow.

19 Stitch a band of pleating round the neck. Cover the seam allowance on the right side with topstitched ribbon, ending in ties at the front.

20 Add ribbon ties at base of yoke. Fine lace edging may be added to the hems of the pleating so that it flutes out.

Victorian Negligee
Size 12. ¼ scale
No seams

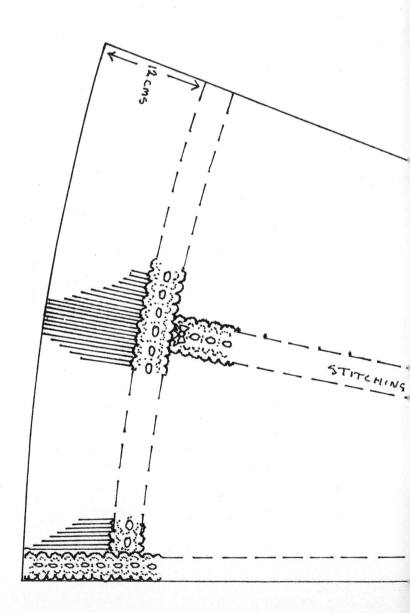

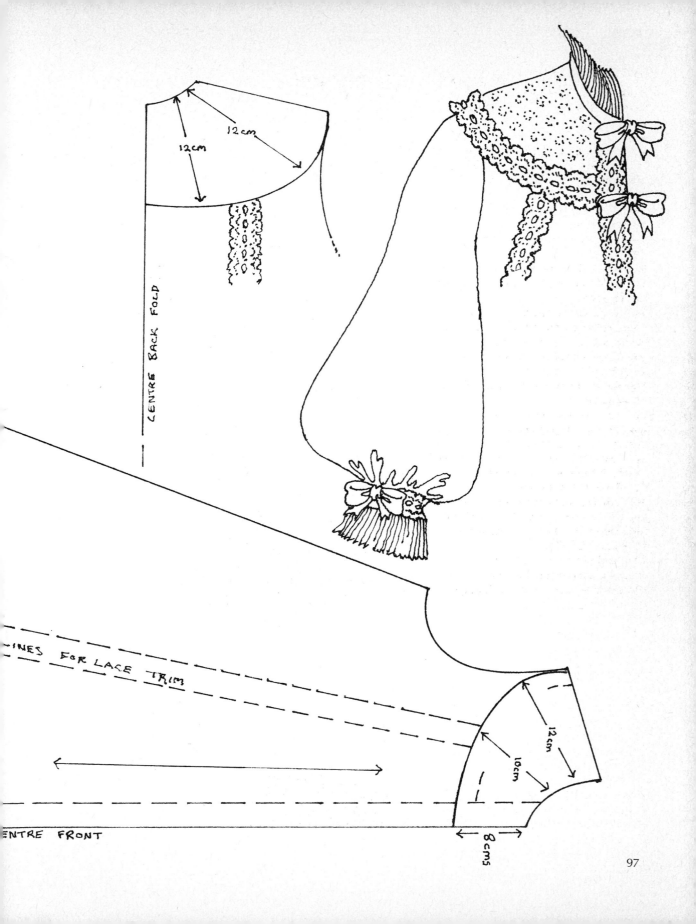

12cm

12cm

CENTRE BACK FOLD

LINES FOR LACE TRIM

CENTRE FRONT

12cm

10cm

8cms

97

WOMAN'S SLEEPSUIT

This simple garment is constructed by joining the French Knicker block (see pages 60–61 to the front and back bodice blocks, then elongating the legs to the required length. The bodice is cut straight across above the bust, has narrow tied rouleau straps and is elasticated at the waist. When made in cotton lawn it will make a simple, comfortable but extremely pretty sleepsuit, but can easily be adapted to evening wear by using silk crêpe de Chine with perhaps a lace trim to give a luxurious and exotic look. Diagram to size 12, but since the garment is loose and elasticated it is quite adaptable in sizing. If a longer girth length (centre front and centre back) is required the waistline should be cut through and extra length added there.

Suggested fabrics:
Broderie anglaise, cotton lawn (plain or printed), silk crêpe de Chine, Japanese silk or satin.

Construction details:
Needles: 9 or 11 according to fabric used as suggested by needle manufacturers on the needle packet.
Thread: mercerized cotton, size 50 or pure silk.
All seams 5mm (¼in) French seams.
Centre back zip.

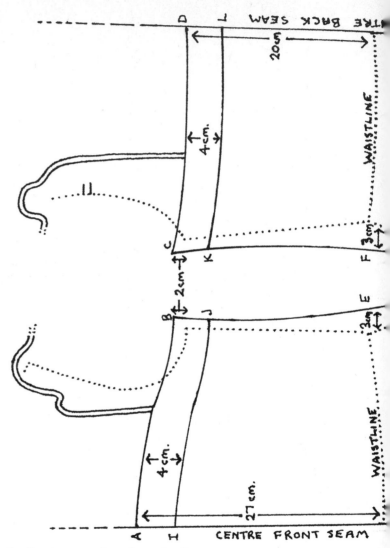

1 Draw round the front and back French Knicker block (see pages 60–61).
2 Add front and back basic bodice block, disregarding the darts and drawing up to the top of the armhole.
3 Measure up the centre front line from the waist for 27cm (10¾in) to point A.
4 Raise the armhole 2cm (¾in) and also move out for 2cm (¾in) to give point B.

5 Repeat stage 4 to give point C on back armhole.
6 Measure 20cm (8in) up from the waist along centre back line to give point D.
7 Join A–B and C–D with gentle curves as in diagram.
8 Measure 3cm (1¼in) outside the waistline to mark points E and F.
9 Measure 2cm (¾in) outside the thigh line to give points G and H.

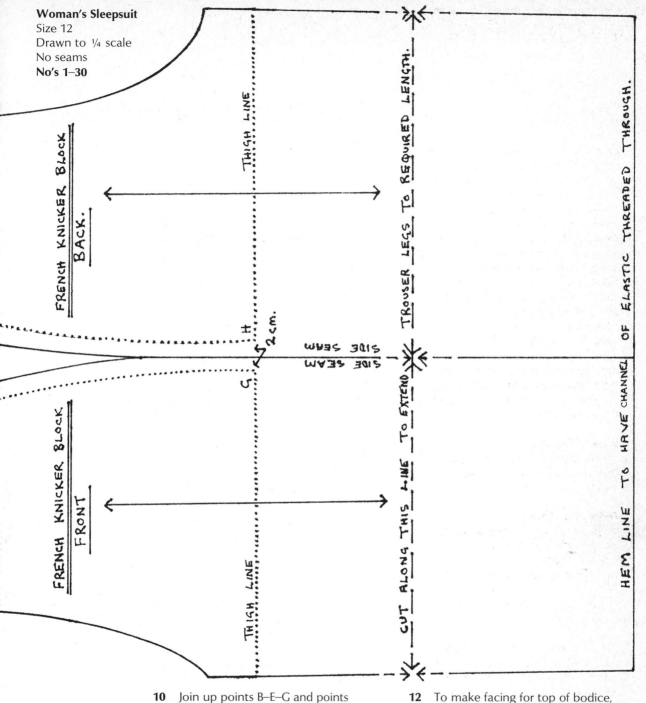

Woman's Sleepsuit
Size 12
Drawn to ¼ scale
No seams
No's 1–30

FRENCH KNICKER BLOCK
BACK.

FRENCH KNICKER BLOCK
FRONT

THIGH LINE

TROUSER LEGS TO REQUIRED LENGTH.

CUT ALONG THIS LINE TO EXTEND

SIDE SEAM

HEM LINE TO HAVE CHANNEL OF ELASTIC THREADED THROUGH.

10 Join up points B–E–G and points C–F–H to give new, wider side seam.
11 Drop side seams and inside leg seams, parallel to each other to the required length. (Remember to add an extra 10cm (4in) for blousing at the ankle.)

12 To make facing for top of bodice, mark a depth of 4cm (1¾in) down and parallel to top line and curve in the second line I–J and K–L. The front facing can be cut out all in one, hence a centre front fold.

13 Before cutting out the pattern, if an opening is required add a 2·5cm (1in) seam allowance down centre back for 16cm (6½in) and 1 cm (½in) seams on all other seams.

14 Cut out two fronts, two backs and the three facings.

15 Stitch side seams using 5mm (¼in) French seams.

16 Stitch inside leg seams using 5mm (¼in) French seams.

17 Stitch down centre front seams, through crutch and up into the centre back to the base of the zip opening, using a 5mm (¼in) French seam.

18 Press in the zip allowance and sew in the zip.

19 Cut the shoulder straps from 3cm (1¼in) wide bias strips so that they are long enough to tie on the shoulders.

20 Make rouleau straps to finished width of 1cm (½in). Pin in position on inside of bodice.

21 Stitch side seams of facing and press open the seam allowances.

22 Press lower edge of facing to wrong side with a 5mm (¼in) seam allowance.

23 Pin facing to inside of top edge of bodice with right side of facing towards inside of garment.

24 Machine 5mm (¼in) seam allowance round top, clip seam and press to right side of garment. The shoulder straps should have been anchored in during this operation.

25 Edge stitch the pressed-in edge of the facing to the right side of the bodice, pressing the centre back seam allowance and also topstitch down on the same line as the zip.

26 Topstitch narrow cotton tape along the waistline on the inside to make a channel for the elastic.

27 Thread narrow elastic around the waist, cut 10cm (4in) short of the required waist measurement.

28 Press a 5mm (¼in) hem around the bottom of the trousers.

29 Repeat with a 1cm (½in) hem so that no raw edge is showing.

30 Edge stitch hem down leaving a 1·5cm (⅝in) gap to allow the ankle elastic to be threaded through.

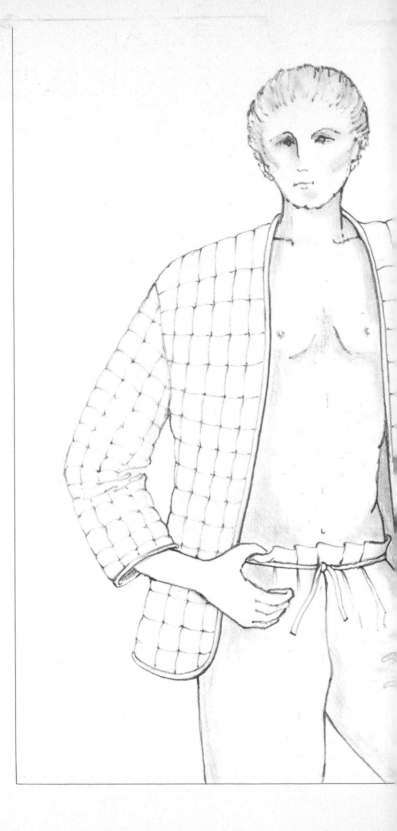

WOMAN'S QUILTED SLEEP JACKET OR EVENING JACKET

This semi-fitted jacket is designed to be worn over the sleepsuit and can be adapted for indoors or outer wear according to the fabric used. Ready-made quilting can now be bought in a variety of materials ranging from man-made fabrics to cotton and viyella. For a more luxurious effect pure silk, satin or brocade could be quilted by the dressmaker to achieve a glamour that would be more suitable for evenings out!
Diagram for size 12 but semi-fitted for an adaptable fit.

Suggested fabrics:
Printed quilted synthetics, quilted cotton, quilted viyella, quilted silk or brocade.

Construction details:
Needles: size 14 or 16
Thread: mercerized cotton size 50. Long machine stitch. All outside edges bound with double folded bias cut strip, 6cm (2½in) wide. Inside seams zigzag edged or the seams bound.

1 Draw around the back block disregarding the waist dart.
2 Transfer the front shoulder dart by drawing in new side dart 20cm (8in) down from armhole to point A and ruling a line to bust point B.
3 Cut along line AB and sellotape the shoulder dart BC together so that line AB opens to give the new dart.
4 Disregard the waist dart.
5 Mark a point 28cm down centre front, to give point D. Draw in the new curve of the V-shaped neck.
6 Measure 6cm (2½in) from the centre front at the hem line to give point E.
7 Curve a line from point E up to waistline to give the new edge.

8 Draw round the straight sleeve block and divide equally into four vertical panels.

9 Cut these dotted lines from the hem to the crown, but not right the way through the crown (this is the same procedure as for the Nightdress chapter see page 78 stages 19–26).

10 Open up the three gaps at the hem for 2cm (¾in) and draw in the new curved hem line. This will give a gentle flare to the sleeve.

11 Cut out the five pattern pieces in the fabric, i.e. two fronts, one back and two sleeves.

Most ready quilted fabrics have a backing already on them, but if this is not the case the jacket will have to be lined, so cut out identical pattern pieces in lining.

12 Stitch the darts, cut down the fold and press open. If the jacket is to be unlined the raw edges should be zigzagged (it is advisable to tack through the stitching lines of darts first).

13 Repeat for the shoulder darts, but do not open since they are too small.

14 Stitch shoulder seams, press open and zigzag edges.

15 Repeat for side seams.

16 Stitch sleeves and stitch into jacket, zigzagging all the raw edges of the seams.

17 The remaining raw edges of the neck, hem and cuffs can now be bound by the bias strip in the same fabric as the Sleep Suit or a contrast. If the jacket is to be lined this should be tacked all the way round the edge of the jacket and the bindings sewn through jacket and lining.

18 Measure round the edge of the jacket and cut the 6cm (2½in) bias strip accordingly.

19 Press the strip in half lengthwise.

20 Starting at the centre back of the hem stitch bias strip to right side of the jacket with the two raw edges level with the raw edge of the jacket (the seam should be 1cm (½in) from the edge).

21 Machine right the way round and finish off ends at centre back by folding the two ends onto the outside.

22 Press the folded strip out towards the edge of the jacket. Fold over all the raw edges and pin to the inside of the jacket. This should leave a 1cm (½in) binding visible on the right side of the jacket.

23 Hand slipstitch the folded edge of the binding to the inside of the jacket.

24 Repeat the binding procedure for the cuffs.

Although the jacket is supposed to be edge to edge, rouleau ties can be added at the waistline at the front.

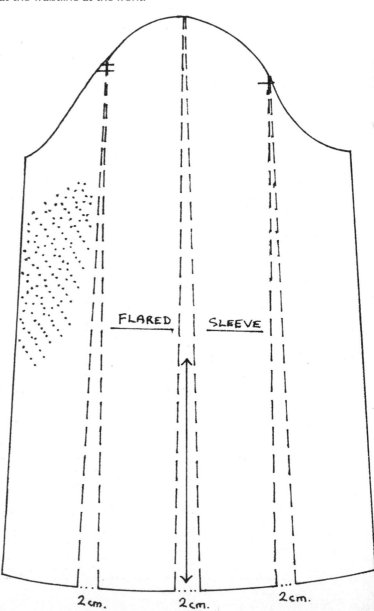

FLARED SLEEVE

2 cm.   2 cm.   2 cm.

Woman's quilted sleep jacket or evening jacket, semi-fitted with flared sleeves, bound edges.
Size 12. Diagram drawn to ¼ scale. No seams

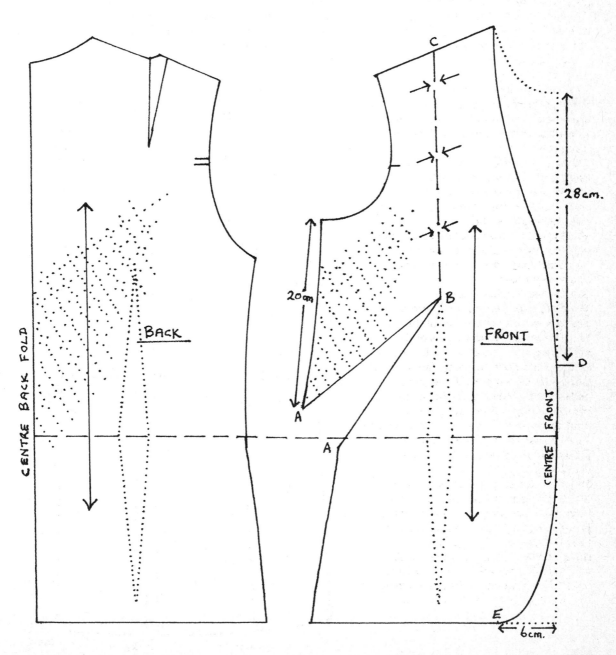

CENTRE BACK FOLD

BACK

FRONT

CENTRE FRONT

20cm

28cm.

6cm.

C

B

A

A

D

E

MAN'S QUILTED SLEEPSUIT

1. THE JACKET

This jacket, luxurious and comfortable, is designed to be worn with gathered silk trousers. An updated version of the smoking jacket, its casual look suits the more relaxed life style of the 70s where a bare torso is quite acceptable, or the jacket can be worn with a silk scarf or even a casual top in the form of a T-shirt. For the man who wants minimum effort but maximum effect this would be perfect for relaxing at home or for social occasions outside. Obviously quilted silk in plain colours would be the most sophisticated, but there is no reason why a print or stripe could not be used. For sleep wear or relaxing at home, no fastening is necessary, but a tie belt in Judo fashion could give it a different dimension.

As for the trousers, it would be an advantage to buy a readymade simple man's unstructured pattern (see page 107) and adapt it to the measurements shown on the diagram.

The method of construction is identical to that of the woman's. However, it has a slightly fitted centre back seam for a more tailored look. It just relies on the combination of fabrics and colours to give it the masculinity and effect that it deserves.

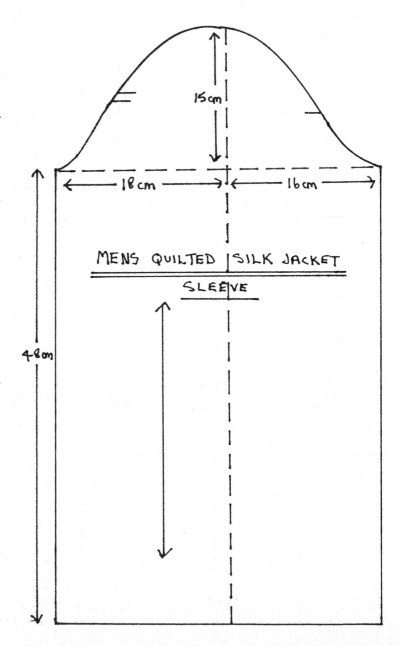

MENS QUILTED SILK JACKET

SLEEVE

15 cm

18 cm

16 cm

48 cm

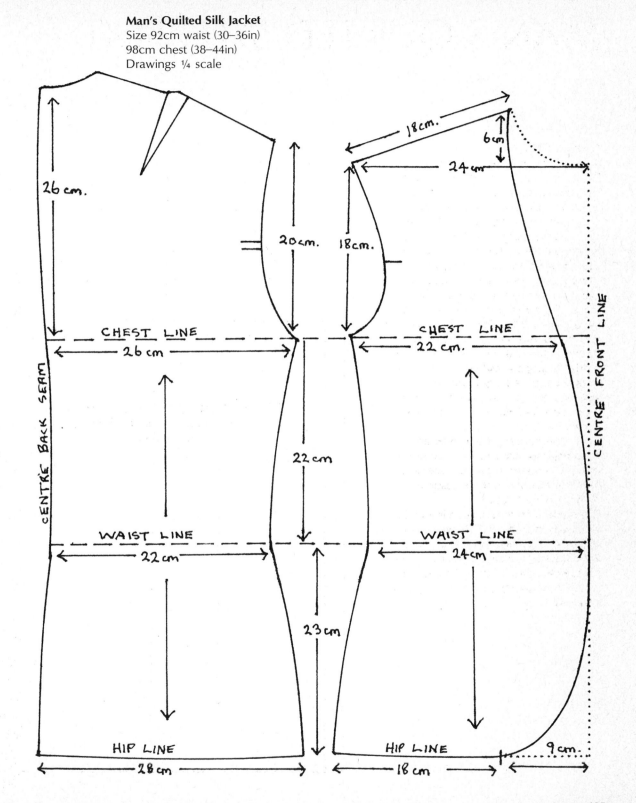

Man's Quilted Silk Jacket
Size 92cm waist (30–36in)
98cm chest (38–44in)
Drawings ¼ scale

26 cm.

18cm.

6cm

24 cm

20cm.

18cm.

CHEST LINE

CHEST LINE

26 cm

22 cm.

CENTRE BACK SEAM

CENTRE FRONT LINE

22 cm

WAIST LINE

WAIST LINE

22 cm

24cm

23 cm

HIP LINE

HIP LINE

9 cm.

28 cm

18 cm

2. THE TROUSERS

These trousers, to be worn with the quilted silk jacket, complete an outfit of minimum fuss with maximum comfort and luxurious ease. The trousers have a gathered elasticated waist and tapering legs. No opening is necessary since the waist is elasticated. To save the drudgery of drawing a pattern from scratch it would be advisable to purchase a readymade trouser pattern and adapt it. All the measurements given are drafted from the central crease lines. This is easily found by folding the pattern piece of each leg in half lengthwise. If less taper to the leg is required simply add extra to the outside leg seam at each side seam at the hem then taper up to the original line. When doing this it is essential that an equal amount is added to each leg or else the hang of the leg will be affected. Size to fit waist 75cm–105cm (30–42in) waist.

Suggested fabrics:
Silk crêpe de Chine, silk twill, silk satin, cotton lawn.

Construction details:
Needles: sizes 9 or 11
Thread: pure silk thread
5mm (¼in) French seams for sides, inside leg and seat seams.

1 Stitch side seams using a 5mm (¼in) French seam. If side pockets are desired they should either be cut in one with the trouser leg or seamed on before the side seam.
2 Repeat for inside leg seams.
3 Stitch the two legs together around seat seam using a 5mm (¼in) French seam.
4 Make a 1·5cm (⅝in) channel around the waist seam by pressing 5mm (¼in) edge to the inside. Press over again and edge stitch down leaving a 1·5cm (⅝in) gap in which to thread the elastic. The elastic should be cut 10cm (4in) shorter than the actual waist measurement.

Man's Elastic Waist Tapered Trousers
To fit waist 76cm–104cm waist.
110cm outside leg. Diagram ¼ scale.

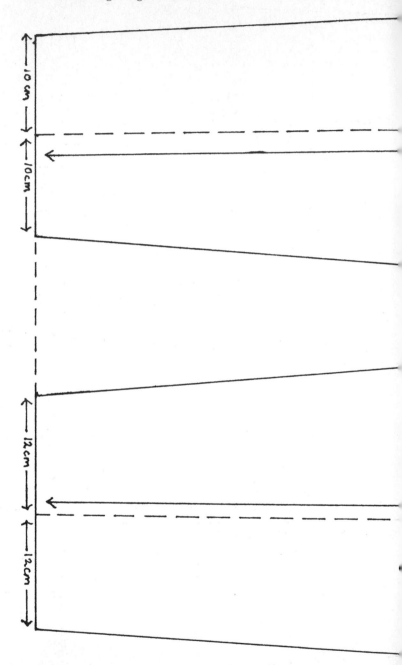

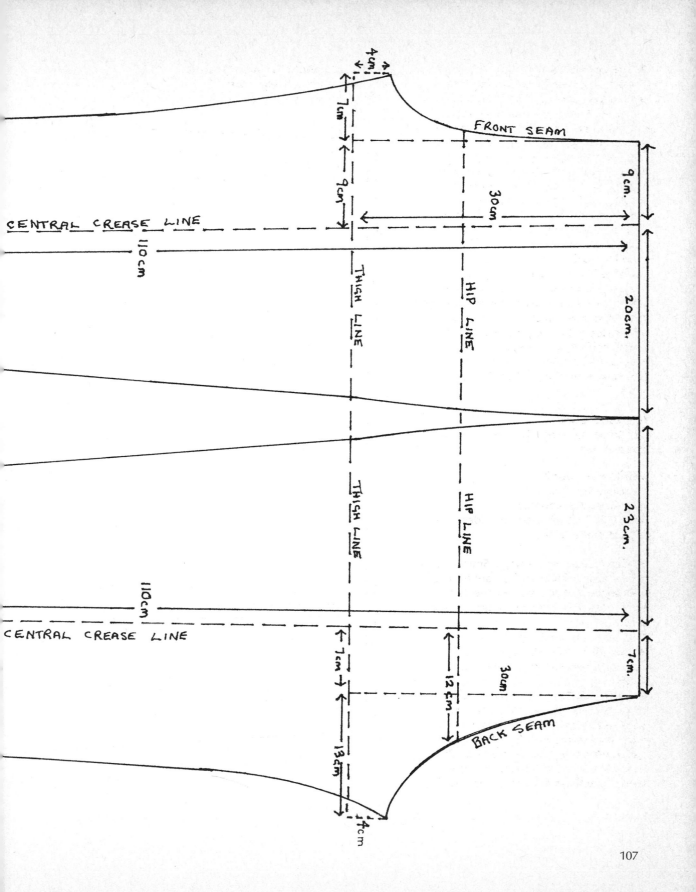

FRONT SEAM

4 cm

7 cm

9 cm

CENTRAL CREASE LINE

110 cm

9 cm

30 cm

20 cm

THIGH LINE

HIP LINE

THIGH LINE

HIP LINE

23 cm

110 cm

CENTRAL CREASE LINE

7 cm

12 cm

30 cm

7 cm

13 cm

BACK SEAM

4 cm

107